Series / Number 07-070

# POOLED TIME SERIES ANALYSIS

**Lois W. Sayrs**
*University of Iowa*

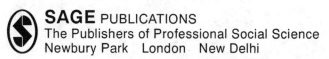

**SAGE** PUBLICATIONS
The Publishers of Professional Social Science
Newbury Park   London   New Delhi

*For information address:*

SAGE Publications, Inc.
2111 West Hillcrest Drive
Newbury Park, California 91320

SAGE Publications Ltd.
28 Banner Street
London EC1Y 8QE
England

SAGE Publications India Pvt. Ltd.
M-32 Market
Greater Kailash I
New Delhi 110 048 India

International Standard Book Number 0-8039-3160-3

Library of Congress Catalog Card No. 89-061129

FIRST PRINTING 1989

When citing a university paper, please use the proper form. Remember
to cite the correct Sage University Paper series title and include the
paper number. One of the following formats can be adapted (depending
on the style manual used):

(1) IVERSEN, GUDMUND R. and NORPOTH, HELMUT (1976)
"Analysis of Variance." Sage University Paper series on Quantitative
Applications in the Social Sciences, 07-001. Beverly Hills: Sage Pubns.

*OR*

(2) Iversen, Gudmund R. and Norpoth, Helmut. 1976. Analysis of Variance. Sage University Paper series on Quantitative Applications in the
Social Sciences, series no. 07-001. Beverly Hills: Sage Pubns.

QA
280
.S29
1989

## CONTENTS

## SERIES EDITOR'S INTRODUCTION*

What is a *pooled time series?* As the phrase implies, *time series* (regular temporal observations on a unit of analysis) are combined with *cross-sections* (observations on a unit of analysis at single time points) to form one data set. The units of analysis may be schools, health organizations, businesses , cities, or states, to name a few. Why do a "pooled analysis"? For one reason, more and more often researchers now have available relevant data collected in both formats. For another, pooling time series and cross-sectional data can greatly boost sample size, making possible analysis that is otherwise highly problematic.

Take a simple example. Professor Broom wishes to account for variation in property crime rates in a sample of 20 American cities. She proposes the following model:

$$C = a + b_1U + b_2L + b_3R + e$$

with the variables, $C$ = city property crime rate, $U$ = unemployment rate, $L$ = law enforcement quality, $R$ = regional location, all measured each year for 15 years. Assuming classical regression assumptions are met, Broom might apply ordinary least squares (OLS) estimation to the above equation 15 times (once for each annual cross-section). And, she might apply OLS another 20 times (once for each city measured over time). Alternatively, assuming that the parameters $(a, b_1, b_2,$ and $b_3)$ are constant across space and time, she might simply prefer to pool the observations and calculate only one regression. This parsimonious procedure would greatly increase the $N$, to 300, and much improve the statistical efficiency of the estimates.

Such an application of OLS follows what Dr. Sayrs labels the *constant coefficients* model of pooled analysis. The principal difficulty with it is the demanding assumption of constant parameters. Less demanding is the *least squares dummy variable* model (sometimes called the *covariance* model), which permits the intercept to vary by time and by cross-section. Still, such dummy variables are substantively meaningless, and greatly reduce the degrees of freedom, with a corresponding loss of statistical power. A possible substitute is the *error components* model (also referred to as the *random coefficient* model by Professor Sayrs), which takes explicit account of cross-sectional and time series disturbances. Nevertheless, the required weighted least squares type-estimation should not be used with a lagged dependent variable on the right-hand side or if the equation is imbedded in a larger simultaneous-equation system. Moreover, the error assumptions may be undermined in the face of serious time series autocorrelation. To go beyond the error components model, Professor Sayrs offers a *structural equation* model, concluding her discussion with remarks on the robustness of estimators in pooled time series analysis.

—*Michael S. Lewis-Beck*
Series Editor

*This volume was initially accepted by the former editors, Richard Niemi and John Sullivan.

# POOLED TIME SERIES ANALYSIS

**LOIS W. SAYRS**
*University of Iowa*

## 1. INTRODUCTION

**This monograph** describes regression analysis for data that are a combination of cross-sections and time series. A time series is a numerical sequence, where the interval between observations on a set of variables $X_t$ and $X_{t+1}$) is constant and fixed (Ostrom, 1978). A cross-section is a unit of analysis at a single point in time for which there exist observations on a set of variables $(X_i \ldots X_n)$. When the variables for a number of different cross-sections are observed over a time span, we refer to the resulting data matrix as a *pooled time series*.[1]

There are many ways to characterize the pooled time series matrix, but the standard characterization is first in terms of the cross-sections, then in terms of the time series. The matrix is configured so that the variation within a cross-sectional unit over time is secondary to the variation between the different cross-sections.

The main advantage to combining cross-sections and time series in this manner is to capture variation across different units in space, as well as variation that emerges over time. We are thus able to describe, analyze, and test hypotheses about outcomes and the processes that generate the outcomes. Pooling is particularly useful in applied research when the length of the time series is abbreviated and/or the sample of cross-sections is modest in size. Often, a single univariate time series is too short for conventional time series techniques. Many time series methods require at least thirty time points and some techniques may require more.[2]

The central purpose of this monograph is to introduce the pooled time series design to readers who already have a basic familiarity with the linear model, regression techniques, and univariate time series estimation.[3] First, the regression model of a pooled time series is examined, followed by various techniques of regression estimation. The monograph is punctuated with examples from various applications of the pooled time series design to problems in the social and behavioral sciences. The format of the monograph combines a full theoretical presentation of the problems of pooled time series with specific applications. For ease in reading and using as a classroom text, sections are identified by upper case letters (A, B, C) to indicate degree of difficulty.

## 2. THEORETICAL DERIVATION OF THE POOLED TIME SERIES MODEL[A]

### Pooling in Application[A]

The combination of cross-sections with time series has been prevalent in applied research and econometric theory since the 1950s.[4] Like many other research designs in the social and behavioral sciences, pooled time series has been closely related to the specific problems for which it was first used. Balestra and Nerlove's (1966) analysis, for example, of the demand for natural gas employs a very simple covariance technique to correct for variation between the cross-sections, but one that is unique to the cross-section, i.e., dummy variables.[5] Such an approach was originally termed "fixed" because the covariation was fixed in an intercept term rather than assumed to vary as a random variable. If allowed to vary randomly, the covariation would simply be part of the overall error in the regression model and somewhat difficult to disentangle from all the other influences on the error in the model. The fixed versus random terminology, however, is somewhat misleading since fixed effects are indeed random effects that may be treated as if they were "fixed" in the sample. As Mundlak's (1978) discussion points out:

> Without a loss in generality, it can be assumed from the outset that the effects are random and view the F[ixed] E[ffects] inference as *conditional* inference, that is, conditional on the effects that are in the sample (emphasis added) [p. 70].

Yet, often the choice between fixed and random effects is not immediately apparent from the sample. Stimson (1985), for example, models issue polarization in the U.S. House of Representatives by fixing the variance between the cross-sections in regional groupings for states. Markus's (1986) paper on electoral choice in presidential elections conditions the variance on a set of instruments for the sample. As long as the error is not hopelessly contaminated from misspecification or correlation with right-hand-side variables, the choice for fixing the variance can actually be a simple one. As Judge et al. (1985) remind us, it is useful to characterize the problem in terms of the correlation between the independent variables and the error when the choice of fixed or random is not clearcut.

If there is the possibility that the dummies and the explanatory variables are correlated, then Judge et al. (1985) recommend a fixed effects approach, that is, an approach to estimation that fixes the error in dummy variables. This is especially true when the number of cases is small.[6] This problem may arise, for example, when explaining recidivism in criminal behavior. Explanatory variables like socioeconomic status, drug use, and type of crime committed could be correlated with a dummy variable such as prison location. The estimate of the effect of location on recidivism will be biased if the error (distribution of residual variance) is assumed to be random when it is in fact dependent or conditional on the location of the prison. The uncontrolled variables could be standardized between prison populations so the $X_i$ continues to have the same relationship to $Y$, but just one of different magnitude and/or direction. It must be noted, however, that when standardization is the chosen course, a new problem emerges in that the actual effect is no longer straightforwardly interpreted. As we shall see in the examples given here, examination of residual variance is an important, if not essential, diagnostic to detecting any sources of contamination in a pooled design.

Since the Balestra and Nerlove (1966) model, many different applications have been made using covariance techniques (e.g., Hibbs, 1976; Zuk and Thompson, 1982). The various needs of specific research contexts within which these and other pooled models have arisen has created a burgeoning applied literature. There is, however, a growing theoretical literature on the use of the model in applied settings (Stimson, 1985) and correction of violated assumptions (cf., Hoch, 1962; Maddala, 1971; Mundlak, 1978; Nerlove, 1971; Wallace and Hussain, 1969). There are now available several econometric texts that are widely used and include a section on pooling (e.g., Amemiya, 1985; Judge et al., 1985; Kmenta, 1971; Maddala, 1977).

## The Pooled Linear Regression Model[A]

A pooled time series can be treated as data that are stacked by cross-section and over time. Table 2.1 shows actual data stacked in a pool. These stacks are sorted first by the variable ACTOR, which is the agent of international conflict, then by TARGET, which is the recipient of the conflict behavior, then by YEAR, which is the year when the conflict behavior took place. This is the *standard* way to stack data for a pooled time series. One could, for example, stack first by YEAR than by ACTOR and TARGET, but the research question should determine the stacking. In Table 2.1 the data is sorted to reflect the uniqueness of each actor in conflict behavior, then each recipient of a conflict action, then the year in which the activity occurred. The kinds of questions these data may be helpful in answering might include the influence of regional location (Western Europe, Africa), Cold War tension (1958-68), or both on the level of conflict among international actors. The research question at hand, however, may require a different stacking. In Chapter 4, when the Least Squares Dummy Variable model is examined, an alternative stacking is presented and compared with the more standard stacking. It should be remembered, however, that the stacking is a direct function of the research question. In this case, the ACTOR and TARGET provide the cross-sectional variation while YEAR provides the variation over time. Additional variables of interest are listed in Table 2.1 to give visual evidence of the variation in this particular data set. The other included variables are ADJUST (number of executive transfers of governing authority) and NETCON (the total amount of international conflict minus the total amount of international cooperation from ACTOR to TARGET).

Let us now consider the data matrix represented in Table 2.1 more theoretically in order to derive the general case and a linear estimator. Begin with the linear model and one explanatory variable. Data for both the $X$ and $Y$ variables extend over $n$ number of cross-sections and $t$ points in time. The cross-sections could be firms, states, cities, Standard Metropolitan Statistical Areas (SMSA), political parties, prison populations, jurisdictions, etc. The pooled model for one case and one variable would take the following form:

$$Y_{nt} = X_{nt}\,\beta_k + u_{nt} \qquad [2.1]$$

where $n = 1....N$ *cross-sections*
and $t = 1....T$ time points.

TABLE 2.1
Data Matrix for Stacks of Pooled Times Series Sorted by ACTOR
(descending), TARGET (descending), and YEAR (ascending)

| Case | Actor | Target | Year | Adjust | Netcon |
|------|-------|--------|------|--------|--------|
| 1 | 750 | 380 | 1950 | 3 | 0.0 |
| 2 | 750 | 380 | 1951 | 0 | 0.0 |
| 3 | 750 | 380 | 1952 | 2 | 0.0 |
| . | . | . | . | . | . |
| . | . | . | . | . | . |
| . | . | . | . | . | . |
| 26 | 750 | 380 | 1975 | 7 | 0.0 |
| 27 | 750 | 020 | 1950 | 3 | 0.0 |
| 28 | 750 | 020 | 1951 | 0 | −8.0 |
| 29 | 750 | 020 | 1952 | 2 | 0.0 |
| . | . | . | . | . | . |
| . | . | . | . | . | . |
| 52 | 750 | 020 | 1975 | 7 | 0.0 |
| 53 | 740 | 651 | 1950 | 3 | 0.0 |
| 54 | 740 | 651 | 1951 | 1 | 0.0 |
| 55 | 740 | 651 | 1952 | 4 | −10.0 |
| . | . | . | . | . | . |
| . | . | . | . | . | . |
| | | . | | . | |
| | | . | | | |
| 910 | 002 | 020 | 1975 | 3 | 0.0 |

For more than one explanatory variable, the model would be modified
in the following way:

$$Y_{nt} = X_{knt}\beta_k + u_{nt} \qquad [2.2]$$

where $k = 1...K$ explanatory variables.
The structure of the data in matrix representation is:

$$Y = y_{11}$$
$$y_{12}$$
$$.$$
$$.$$
$$y_{it}$$
$$.$$
$$.$$
$$y_{nt}$$

$$X = \begin{array}{cccccc} x_{11.1} & x_{11.2} & x_{11.3} & \ldots & x_{11k} \\ x_{12.1} & x_{12.2} & x_{12.3} & \ldots & x_{12k} \\ \cdot & \cdot & \cdot & & \cdot \\ \cdot & \cdot & \cdot & & \cdot \\ x_{it.1} & x_{it.2} & x_{it.3} & \ldots & x_{it.k} \\ \cdot & \cdot & \cdot & & \cdot \\ \cdot & \cdot & \cdot & & \cdot \\ x_{nt.1} & x_{nt.2} & x_{nt.3} & \cdots & x_{nt.k} \end{array}$$

$$U = \begin{array}{c} u_{11} \\ u_{12} \\ \cdot \\ \cdot \\ u_{it} \\ \cdot \\ \cdot \\ u_{nt} \end{array}$$

and

$$\beta = \begin{array}{c} \beta_1 \\ \cdot \\ \cdot \\ \beta_i \\ \cdot \\ \cdot \\ \beta_k \end{array}$$

Therefore:

$$\Omega = \begin{array}{ccccc} U(u^2_{11}) & \ldots & U(u_{11}u_{it}) & \ldots & U(u_{11}u_{nt}) \\ \cdot & & \cdot & & \cdot \\ U(u_{it}u_{11}) & \ldots & U(u^2_{it}) & \ldots & U(u_{it}u_{nt}) \\ \cdot & & \cdot & & \cdot \\ U(u_{nt}u_{11}) & \ldots & U(u_{nt}u_{it}) & \ldots & U(u^2_{nt}) \end{array}$$

In the pooled time series design, we begin by retaining the assumptions of the standard linear model:

$$E\,(u_{nt}) = 0 \text{ for all } n. \tag{2.3}$$

$$V\,(u_{nt}) = \sigma^2 \text{ for all } n. \tag{2.4}$$

$$COV\,(u_{it}u_{jt}) = 0 \text{ for any } i,\,j,\,t. \tag{2.5}$$

$$COV\,(u_{it}x_{it}) = 0 \text{ for any } i,\,t. \tag{2.6}$$

$$U_{nt} \approx N\,(0,\,\sigma^2). \tag{2.7}$$

In a pool of time series, these assumptions are easily violated. When, for example, both stochastic and non-stochastic variables are included in the regression equation, the expected value of the error is not zero and variance is not $\sigma^2$. Thus, to begin to estimate a pooled model under these conditions requires first correcting for the inclusion of non-stochastic variables. Because the ordinary concerns of regression, such as nonconstant variance, are now compounded from the potential correlation from one time point to another, a concern more typical of time series analysis, both assumptions 2.5 and 2.6 are easily violated in pooled estimation. The pool creates the opportunity for error to be contaminated from correlation between time points within one cross-section. Contamination also arises from correlation in the error from different cross-sections at the *same* time point or from different cross-sections *and* different time points. The effects from the cross-sections are referred to as *unit effects,* and these unit effects can be isolated from other sources of contamination or felt in combination with other sources of contamination, such as serial correlation. The example of stacks in Table 2.1 reveals by simple visual inspection that some variables such as GDP or TRADE might contaminate error with autoregression within a cross-section. Heteroscedasticity is more difficult to detect without a scatterplot of the residuals.

The assumptions that undergird the model of 2.2 suggest that there is no relationship between the time points within a cross-section or time points between the cross-sections and that there is no relationship between the cross-sections within a time point or between time points. For example, there might be no theoretical connection between the cross-section "England" and the cross-section "France" in the time point "1942"; "England" in "1942" and "England" in "1943"; or "England" in "1942" and "France" in "1943." On the other hand, there may very well be a theoretical relationship among these different units and time points, but it is not specified in the regression model. This misspecification is captured only in the error and, as such, is a source of contamination of the regression estimates in a pooled time series.

A natural way to proceed then is to specify the error so that this relationship, however simple or complex, is captured. We would like to identify the source of contamination as "time," "cross-section," or "both." But identifying the source of the error is not enough. We would like to be able to discern whether the effect of the $X_i$ on $Y_{nt}$ is the same for all cross-sections, one that differs in magnitude but not direction, one that differs in direction but not magnitude, or one that differs in both magnitude and direction for various cross-sections. These differences in magnitude and direction are used as the theoretical basis on which to estimate the linear effect of the $X_i$ on the $Y_{nt}$. Four different models are considered in detail to characterize the relationship between $X_i$ and $Y_{nt}$. The four models reflect alternative assumptions about the relationship between the right-hand-side variables and the error.

## Four Models of Pooling[A]

There are numerous ways to characterize the relationship between the right-hand-side variables and the error in a pooled time series. Here, four models are presented that have a basis in standard regression analysis and so should be relatively familiar to the reader. Each reflects unique assumptions, but the effort is made to ground each in econometric theory in order to bring into full view the weaknesses and strengths of each model. The four models are not exhaustive, but more importantly, as we will be reminded throughout the discussion, the theoretical question itself is the first, best guide to model selection.

The first model is called the *constant coefficients model* because the coefficients that characterize the effect of the $X_i$ on $Y_{nt}$ are the same or are held constant for all cross-sections. There are no variations in the sample that would undermine the *constant* relationship that the independent variables have with the dependent variable. The second model is a Least Squares Dummy Variable (LSDV) model, which recognizes the nonconstant variation in a relatively simple way. This model captures variation unique to the cross-section in an intercept that varies from cross-section to cross-section. In its simplest form, the direction of the relationship remains constant for all cross-sections, but the LSDV model is easily extended to include interaction effects. The third model is often called an *error components model* because the variation in the magnitude and the direction of the relationship among the cross-sections is assumed to be random but captured and specified in the error term explicitly. There are some interesting and useful variations on this model that permit its extension to a qualitative dependent variable, for example. The fourth model is the *structural equation model,* which recasts the research question as a specification problem where omitted effects from time and variation among cross-sections are modeled explicitly in a set of structural equations rather than included as error.

These four models reflect different approaches to estimation in a pool, but there is still no substitute for the basis of comparability among the units. Pooling becomes a very difficult exercise when the theoretical foundation of the regression model is weak. Weakness in a model may emanate from many sources, including poor data (too few data points; too many missing values; a sample that is not distributed normally), insufficient theory to guide the statistical tests, inadequate specification of the empirical model, and models that simply fit the data poorly. Each model has its attractions and drawbacks, but there is no *correct* way to estimate in a pool. Discerning different causal relationships is somewhat more perplexing than it sounds because it could easily call into question the original justification for grouping independent cross-sections (aggregating) as an aspect of the research design. A recent paper by Achen (1986) considers some of the more dangerous implications of aggregation in regression. And for those interested in cross-national comparisons, one observer argues:

> Comparing China or Taiwan, for example, in the same regression analysis may well have the same effect on your regression coefficients as weighting your analysis by including three Indias, two Benins, and a half dozen Japans. Regression coefficients . . . are only meaningful if the data base contains observations on comparable units [Ward, 1987].

The author is right to be concerned with the effect of incorrect aggregation over units of analysis (cross-sections) that are fundamentally not comparable. *Pooling is not a solution to this problem.* Indeed, a pooled design will quickly reveal noncomparability because the disturbance vector will not fit a set of realistic assumptions about the data.

## Preliminary Diagnostics and Residual Analysis[A]

Given a theory and an empirical model, an early part of estimation in a pooled design is a kind of water-testing. Despite how attractive the design may be to applied research, if there is a weak theoretical base or poor data it is better to uncover these aspects early so that should they be intractable, an alternative research design can be specified. It cannot be overemphasized that pooling is a design question first and foremost. No amount of econometric theory can substitute for a weak theoretical foundation or bad data.

But suppose sufficient theory and data are thought to be in hand. Then consider a vector of residuals from the regression in 2.2. In this example, $Y$ is the net level of international conflict (conflict minus cooperation) from an actor to a target nation and $X_i$ is the number of political turnovers in the executive for the actor i. This vector is given in Figure 2.1. We examine the residuals to discriminate between the effects of the cross-sections, the effects of time, and the effects of other things that are random but related to both the cross-sections and time.

It is clear from visual inspection that the variance in these residuals is not constant, but we are particularly concerned with the degree to which these residuals are contaminated. The contamination appears to be from the inclusion of two *classes* of cross-sections. The first class falls above the 770 mark on the level of conflict while the second class seems unable to reach far above 270 in net conflict. There is clearly some systematic variability among the cross-sections on the level of net international conflict, perhaps indicating a relationship between internal and international conflict that not only differs among the cross-sections in magnitude, but in direction as well. From this example, it is quite easy to see that many different regression lines could be fit through these data in addition to the two mentioned using net conflict as a basis of distinction. Let us next examine the residual variance in order to discern the exact source of contamination. These diagnostics are given in Table 2.2.

Table 2.2 offers additional evidence of contamination in the least squares residual vector. Cross-section numbers 23 and 13 are by far

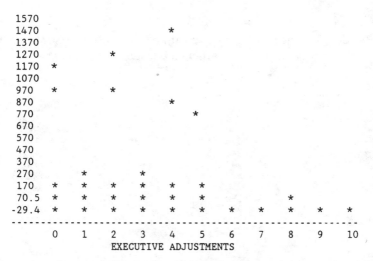

```
1570
1470                               *
1370
1270                  *
1170    *
1070
 970    *             *
 870                        *
 770                           *
 670
 570
 470
 370
 270        *        *
 170    *   *    *    *    *    *
70.5    *   *    *    *    *    *                *
-29.4   *   *    *    *    *    *    *    *    *    *    *
       ---------------------------------------------------------
        0   1    2    3    4    5    6    7    8    9    10
                    EXECUTIVE ADJUSTMENTS
```

**Figure 2.1: Scatterplot for Residuals from Regression of the Net Level of International Conflict on Executive Adjustments**

and away outliers where the residual variance is in the thousands. Cross-section numbers 6, 18, and 32 are also very high in variance, but only in the hundreds. We can see that the least squares solution to this problem will yield biased and inefficient results because the variance is far from constant across the different cross-sections.

The first judgment confronting the researcher is to consider the comparability of the cross-sections. Are these 35 cross-sections truly comparable? Does it make sense to drop the outliers at this stage of research? In Chapter 7, a technique will be introduced to assist the researcher in discounting the effects of some outlying residuals should he/she believe firmly that their inclusion is theoretically warranted. For heuristic purposes at this point in the discussion, we shall assume inclusion is warranted and continue with the example.

One solution to the problem of variability, assuming the units are comparable, is to standardize all the data by scoring them on a standard scale. Since the coefficient of interest, however, is no longer neatly interpretable as the change in the level of international conflict for a one-unit change in internal conflict, it is preferable to retain the unscored data but adjust the coefficient to reflect nonconstant variance. This adjustment can be derived in many ways, but only four general ways are discussed here. The query that guides us is: Which model will best characterize the relationship we observe in the residu-

TABLE 2.2

Residual Variance for Thirty-five Cross-Sections from Regression of
Net International Conflict on Executive Adjustments

| Unit | Actor | Target | Residual Variance |
|------|-------|--------|-------------------|
| 1 | 750 | 380 | 13.8224 |
| 2 | 750 | 020 | 29.3656 |
| 3 | 740 | 651 | 25.1827 |
| 4 | 740 | 255 | 13.7786 |
| 5 | 740 | 225 | 16.8304 |
| 6 | 740 | 002 | 449.0861 |
| 7 | 390 | 325 | 101.9652 |
| 8 | 390 | 230 | 23.0046 |
| 9 | 390 | 220 | 91.5050 |
| 10 | 225 | 820 | 25.5834 |
| 11 | 225 | 740 | 23.2526 |
| 12 | 225 | 020 | 25.1159 |
| 13 | 220 | 616 | 5451.5669 |
| 14 | 220 | 580 | 16.3411 |
| 15 | 220 | 450 | 19.7340 |
| 16 | 220 | 437 | 20.5500 |
| 17 | 220 | 390 | 132.0363 |
| 18 | 220 | 225 | 1918.9624 |
| 19 | 220 | 211 | 21.1430 |
| 20 | 200 | 820 | 102.8678 |
| 21 | 200 | 780 | 23.3867 |
| 22 | 200 | 713 | 71.0449 |
| 23 | 200 | 352 | 4674.1855 |
| 24 | 200 | 110 | 49.4006 |
| 25 | 200 | 091 | 17.1338 |
| 26 | 093 | 092 | 56.4215 |
| 27 | 093 | 091 | 97.8335 |
| 28 | 020 | 750 | 62.0144 |
| 29 | 020 | 732 | 20.4390 |
| 30 | 020 | 225 | 18.3354 |
| 31 | 020 | 002 | 141.3418 |
| 32 | 002 | 740 | 889.6711 |
| 33 | 002 | 255 | 1846.7079 |
| 34 | 002 | 094 | 16.5691 |
| 35 | 002 | 020 | 222.5420 |

pooled
Durbin-Watson
d = .835
Bartlett's M = 4789.15
Goldfeld-Quandt R = 10.129

als? Let us begin to answer this question with the constant coefficients model.

# 3. THE CONSTANT COEFFICIENTS MODEL[A]

In the constant coefficients model, we assume that all the coefficients are the same for each cross-section in the pool. The disturbance vector for a given cross-section might follow a first-order autoregressive process *or* be heteroscedastic, but the variance cannot be both decaying over time (autoregression) and nonconstant (heteroscedastic). *This point cannot be overemphasized.* Autoregression can only be detected after the heteroscedasticity is controlled for. The Durbin-Watson statistic cannot be used as a test statistic under the assumptions of the standard linear model in the case of a pooled design (Stimson, 1985).[7] This test statistic assumes that there is no contamination from heteroscedasticity. The appropriate statistic for a pool must recognize the uniqueness of each cross-section. The pooled Durbin-Watson d statistic can be used to detect autoregression. This is a statistic that estimates an average autoregression given the cross-sections. The Durbin-Watson statistic is calculated for each cross-section and then averaged. The regular Durbin-Watson d yields an estimate of the amount of autoregression in a single time series. As the statistic approaches the number 2, there is less autoregression. Since the pooled Durbin-Watson d is simply an average of all the time series in the pool, as the pooled statistic approximates the number 2, the less autoregression, *on average,* there is in the pool. An alternative, yet less appealing statistic, is the Durbin-Watson d calculated cross-section by cross-section. The drawback to this alternative is that it is not useful in drawing conclusions about autoregression on the pooled series, only on independent series. To that extent, it might be used as an additional diagnostic for the autoregressive tendencies of independent time series.

## Estimating the Constant Coefficients Model[A]

Consider the following linear regression model:

$$Y_{nt} = X_{nt} \beta_k + u_{nt} \qquad [3.1]$$

where $Y_{nt}$ = the level of net dyadic international conflict from actor to target
and $X_{nt}$ = the level of internal conflict of the actor
for $n = (1 \ldots N)$ dyadic cross sections.
and $t = (1 \ldots T)$ time points.

From the residual analysis in Chapter 2 we can now test for autoregression and heteroscedasticity. It is of most use to us in this case if we do not have to specify the *exact* form that the heteroscedasticity must take, but it is always a good idea to test against a first-order autoregressive process. Higher order processes and other forms of correlation, such as a moving average process, are relatively rare. More empirical attention is paid to the AR(1) process precisely because it is so prevalent in application. There is no reason to exclude higher order processes or a moving average process from test procedures should these processes be suspected. These processes can be tested for specifically.

Why is the specific form of nonconstant variance so important to correct estimation in a pooled design? Under the ordinary conditions of estimation, heteroscedasticity will lead to inefficient estimates and autoregression will lead to biased estimates under least squares assumptions. These problems are compounded by pooling and so the contamination can be very severe, producing meaningless estimates. Table 2.2 revealed that the autocorrelation in these sample data appears to follow a first-order autoregressive process (AR (1)). The pooled $d$ for these data = .935 for k = 2 (including the constant). Given 34 degrees of freedom, the $d_l$ = 1.39 and the $d_u$ = 1.51. We reject the null hypothesis of no AR(1), whether it may be positive or negative autoregression. The estimates in Table 2.2 were derived by controlling for heteroscedasticity so the autoregression detected at this stage is not artifactual of nonconstant variance in the cross-sections.

## Correcting for Autoregression[A]

In equation 3.1 consider the following assumption:

$$u_{it} = \rho_i u_{t-1} + e_{it} \qquad [3.2]$$

where $e_{nt} \approx N(0, \sigma^2_{ui})$
and $U(u_{i,\,t-1} e_{jt}) = 0$ for all $i, j, t$.

This assumption describes the error as following a first-order autoregressive process.[8] To characterize autoregression in a pool, we need to elaborate slightly. By substitution then,

$$e = \begin{matrix} \sigma^2_1 P_1 & 0\ldots\ldots\ldots & & 0 \\ 0 & & & \cdot \\ \cdot & & \sigma^2_i P_i & \cdot \\ \cdot & & & \cdot \\ 0 & & & \sigma^2_n P_n \end{matrix}$$

and

$$P_i = \begin{matrix} 1 & \rho_i & o^2_i & \ldots & & \rho^{t-1}_i \\ \rho_i & 1 & o_i & \ldots & & \rho^{t-2}_i \\ \rho^2_i & & 1 & & & \cdot \\ \cdot & & & 1 & & \cdot \\ \cdot & & & & 1 & \cdot \\ \rho^{t-1} & & o^{t-2}_i & & & 1 \end{matrix}$$

According to Kmenta (1971:510), if the value of the parameter $\rho$ is allowed to vary from one cross section to another, then:
$U(u_{it}u_{is}) = \rho^{t-s}\sigma^2_i$ for $t \geq s$
and
$U(u_{it}u_{js}) = 0$ for $i \neq j$.

Now redefine the regression model in equation 3.1 as follows:

$$Y^*_{it} = Y_{it} - \rho_{i,t-1} \qquad [3.1a]$$

$$X^*_{it} = X_{it} - \rho_{i,t-1} \qquad [3.1b]$$

$$U^*_{it} = U_{it} - \rho_{i,t-1} \qquad [3.1c]$$

For $t = (2, 3 \ldots T)$ time points
and $i = (1, 2 \ldots N)$ cross-sections.

$\rho$ is obtained from the OLS estimates correcting for heteroscedasticity. Before we define the OLS estimator we shall use in the constant coefficients model, let us consider how we might test for heteroscedastic errors and, if necessary, incorporate nonconstant variance into the OLS regression.

# Heteroscedasticity[A]

Many tests are available to detect heteroscedastic errors, but two of the better known, widely used and simple to calculate tests are Goldfeld and Quandt's (1965) test and Bartlett's (1937) test. A related test is Theil's (1971) ratio test, but its similarity to the Goldfeld-Quandt test makes its inclusion here somewhat redundant.[9] Both the Goldfeld-Quandt test and the Bartlett test are similar in that they test against the null hypothesis that the variance of the disturbances is constant. The alternative hypothesis varies from test to test. The Bartlett test does not incorporate increasing or decreasing variance, while the Goldfeld-Quandt test controls for nondecreasing variance. In a pooled regression, we can test for nonconstant variance for a single point in time, for nonconstant variance within a cross-section, and/or for nonconstant variance in the full pool with respect to time.

Depending on the source of contamination, either a cross-section or a time point may serve as the discriminating axis. If a time point, for example, the variable YEAR in the conflict data, is suspected as a source of contamination, some simple visual inspection techniques as well as more sophisticated tests are available to detect it. YEAR might be contaminated from the influences of election cycles or war years, making the level of conflict increase or decrease accordingly. First, the standard stacking of time series where the file is sorted by cross-section then by year will not clearly reveal influences from YEAR. The file structure must be re-sorted to reflect first year, then cross-section. We first sort the pool by time point (year), then by cross section, so that the first *case* is a time point that contains observations on $k$ variables for $n$ cross-sections. We can plot NET CONFLICT against YEAR to assess the influence of this variable or nonconstant variance. Figure 3.1 shows the scatterplot for the residuals from the regression of NETCON on ADJUST plotted against YEAR. Visually, we can inspect this plot for particular outliers that might undermine the nonconstant variance assumption. We see, for example, in Figure 3.1 that there are about seven outliers in the early years of this data set, most likely caused by specific actors in the set whose variance in the dependent variable NETCON was particularly high. Using two of the statistical tests mentioned above, namely the Bartlett test and the Goldfeld-Quandt test, we can determine the extent to which YEAR, or if we so desire the cross-sections (ACTOR), contaminate the residual variance.

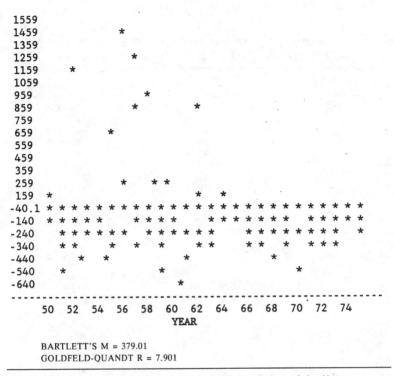

```
1559
1459              *
1359
1259                 *
1159        *
1059
959                  *
859              *        *
759
659         *
559
459
359
259              *    * *
159   *                  *    *
-40.1 * * * * * * * * * * * * * * * * * * * * * * * * *
-140  * * * *    * * * *      * * * * * *    * * * *
-240    * * * * *   * * * * *    * * * * * * *    *
-340    * *    *    *    *    * *    * *    *   * * *
-440      *   *         *              *
-540   *              *                  *
-640                 *
      ----------------------------------------------------
      50  52  54  56  58  60  62  64  66  68  70  72  74
                          YEAR
```

BARTLETT'S M = 379.01
GOLDFELD-QUANDT R = 7.901

**Figure 3.1: Scatterplot for Residuals from Regression of the Net Level of International Conflict on Executive Adjustments (Year Sort).**

Table 3.1 shows results for both the Bartlett test and the Goldfeld-Quandt test on the conflict data sorted by YEAR. The results of these tests for the standard stacking of the series (ACTOR) is in Table 2.2. Table 2.2 utilizes the cross-section as the source of contamination, and both tests suggest that the null hypothesis be rejected in favor of the alternative, i.e., heteroscedasticity. When the year, however, is considered as a source of contamination, the evidence is less clear. The Bartlett test reported in Table 3.1 reveals heteroscedasticity, but the stronger test against nondecreasing variance shows that the variance is inconclusive (Goldfeld-Quandt test). In this case, the researcher may choose to run further diagnostics on year as a source of contamination. More specific treatment of heteroscedasticity and these tests to detect its presence are taken up in Chapter 7, along with other techniques to improve estimation in a pool.

TABLE 3.1
Residual Variance for Twenty-six Years from Regression of Net
International Conflict on Executive Adjustments

| Unit | Year | Residual Variance |
|------|------|-------------------|
| 1 | 1950 | 76.1024 |
| 2 | 1951 | 590.1638 |
| 3 | 1952 | 1869.7269 |
| 4 | 1953 | 384.9070 |
| 5 | 1954 | 757.2788 |
| 6 | 1955 | 524.2492 |
| 7 | 1956 | 2563.2979 |
| 8 | 1957 | 2911.2148 |
| 9 | 1958 | 1316.2859 |
| 10 | 1959 | 496.8330 |
| 11 | 1960 | 99.5706 |
| 12 | 1961 | 1681.5075 |
| 13 | 1962 | 246.2833 |
| 14 | 1963 | 247.8992 |
| 15 | 1964 | 112.0592 |
| 16 | 1965 | 33.9954 |
| 17 | 1966 | 214.8635 |
| 18 | 1967 | 194.3805 |
| 19 | 1968 | 192.0038 |
| 20 | 1969 | 220.9635 |
| 21 | 1970 | 369.0769 |
| 22 | 1971 | 192.1163 |
| 23 | 1972 | 269.6541 |
| 24 | 1973 | 442.9089 |
| 25 | 1974 | 64.1503 |
| 26 | 1975 | 107.2316 |

BARTLETT'S M = 379.01
GOLDFELD-QUANDT R = 7.901

## Limitations of the Constant Coefficient Model[A]

The constant coefficients model is a rather restrictive model for a
pooled time series because it assumes that the relationship between
the explanatory variables and the dependent variable is the same for
all cross-sections and time points. Yet, it does not assume constant
variance or uncorrelated error. It assumes only that these contaminating effects are random to all cross-sections and are indeed captured in
the error. Therefore, corrections, such as specifying an autoregressive
structure to the error, are still appropriate.

There are several attractive aspects of the constant coefficients
model. First, one need not apply a more complicated technique than
ordinary least squares to derive estimates. Second, the simplicity of

the model also forces the researcher to "stay close" to the data—uncover anomalies in the residuals, run more robust tests against autoregression and heteroscedasticity to establish the reliability of the estimates. Third, in the absence of a perfectly specified model, the constant coefficients model will be less likely to produce artificial estimates. The simplicity of ordinary least squares permits relatively easy detection of mistaken assumptions and incorrect (or absent) theory. This model is also attractive because it provides a benchmark against which other, more sophisticated models can be measured.

Yet, there are also certain drawbacks to the constant coefficient model. A very serious weakness is the inability of the model to distinguish variance unique to independent cross-sections or theoretically meaningful groups of cross-sections. For example, the cross-sections "France" and "England" might contribute to the disturbance vector in unique ways or as members of another group called "allies." In the case above where the two heteroscedasticity tests revealed different results, we cannot be content under the assumptions of the constant coefficient model that we have not omitted an important grouped effect such as "war years" or "Cold War" or "OPEC effect."

The constant coefficients model would never recognize this contribution directly because the error cannot be disaggregated any further than one error structure for the entire pool. Second, when the pool contains a large number of cross-sections, the assumption that the relationship between $X_i$ and $Y$ will be the same for all cross-sections is simply unrealistic. Applying this model may be a simple procedure available on any mainframe (and now micro) computer where little more is required than a familiarity with a statistical package program (such as SAS or SPSS), but this model requires the researcher to run test after test, cross-section by cross-section, make corrections, retest the specification, and so on. In short, while the model is simple, it needs a great deal of adjustment in a pool. This may be the model of choice for many research problems where the theory is slight, the data less than totally reliable, and the acceptable range for parameter estimates unknown *a priori*. It is the very simplicity of the model that makes it elegant, but the adjustments are very often *ad hoc,* lacking in theoretical depth. Thus, it is not a simple matter to test hypotheses of interest.

# 4. THE LSDV MODEL[A]

The constant coefficient model treats the pool of time series as if there were one effect that could fit all cross-sections in the pool. It is easy to see that this assumption is not well suited to empirical research. When the residual analysis shows heteroscedastic errors, the relevant question to ask is whether these errors reflect one effect but with different variance or different effects of both magnitude and direction. Consider, for example, a pool of voting behavior for fifty different states in the United States or a pool of crime statistics for twenty SMSAs. Each of these examples is likely to produce heteroscedastic errors because it is not plausible to assume that the variance over the full pool is constant. One of the best ways to manage nonconstant variance in a pool is by introducing a fixed value that represents the variance unique to the cross-section and conditional on the sample. Conditional is used in this sense to imply that should another sample be generated, the sample uniqueness might alter the estimates within a range of error. A simple way to condition the variance is accomplished in least squares by using a dummy variable.

## Heteroscedasticity and Unit Effects[A]

Let us return to the residuals in Figure 2.1. These residuals reveal graphic evidence of heteroscedasticity. The error in Figure 2.1 is related to the cross-sections, the units of analysis. Taken together, these independent sources of contamination combine to create heteroscedasticity, but separately they represent the unique effects of each unit of analysis on the full pool. For this reason, the contaminant effects of the cross-sections under least squares assumptions can be characterized as *unit effects*. Assume for the moment that the error is not contaminated from effects across time, i.e., from time point to time point, but only that the variance is not constant across space. Each case has unique variance. We could run separate models for each cross-section to derive estimates of the effect of executive adjustments (changes in leadership) on international conflict. This approach, however, assumes that the error created by each cross-section is independent of the error created by other cross-sections. The nonconstant variance may be indicative of independence in the cross-sections, or it may simply reflect a single theoretical thrust, which is observed in varying degrees of magnitude and/or direction. For example, the residuals in Figure 2.1 may reflect the effect of "power," "wealth," "development," or some other underlying dimension of comparability. The importance of this underlying theoretical dimension is that the effect can be used to reestimate the regression model but controlling for the nonconstant variance.

Let us examine another example to clarify the impact of unit effects on pooled time series. In this example, the years are the units of analysis, and so we are not interested in variation over time as an explanation of, in this case, presidential popularity but rather treat each year as an independent source of information on attitudes toward the president and the job he is doing.[10] Each year of data contains several observations taken over the course of the year that are captured in the variable called MONTH. Thus, time series variation might emerge from month to month. The years reflect what are essentially unit effects because, in this stacking of the data, the unit of analysis is the year in which the poll was taken.

Examine Figure 4.1 for these unit effects from time. The residuals in this figure reflect the unique contribution of specific time periods. These are *particular* influences over the entire pool of cases for particular time periods that do correspond to specific administrations, i.e., the Truman and Ford administrations, to be precise. The low points in approval might emerge from unique events that negatively affect presidential popularity, e.g., the Korean War or the Nixon pardon. Over the course of the time span reflected in these data, there may have been, in addition to these particular effects, numerous systematic effects through time, e.g., elections that contaminate the residuals and violate the least squares assumption of constant variance. For example, the low points in popularity are not isolated but occur in clusters, which suggests some *drag* relative to popularity. An effect from one time point may contaminate another if only at low points in popularity. The effects of unpopularity, in other words, might last longer than the effects of popularity, and such a situation clearly violates the standard regression assumption of independence. The unique effects will be systematically captured by a dummy variable while other influences, which are more difficult to pin down, may continue to contaminate the error because they are interactive or compounded effects. These effects can plague a time series as "generational effect," i.e., changes in the observed value as a function of maturation,

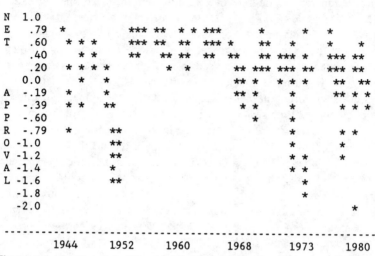

**Figure 4.1: Scatterplot of Presidential Popularity (Net Approval) by Year**

or as *zeitgeist* effects, i.e., changes in observed values as a function of "the spirit of the times."

The LSDV model uses an intercept to capture the effects unique to the cross-sections and those that might be unique to time. The pool permits us to treat the unique effects of time as if time were a surrogate for systematic effects observed in time. Some time periods are systematically influential on the error just as the influence from cross-sections can be systematic or random. We have not made any assumptions about *correlation in time* such as first-order autoregression, only that there might be an influence on the variance from time. This problem frequently reveals itself in the form of seasonal shifts or adjustments, e.g., consumer expenditures at Christmas time, military expenditures during wartime, or polls when particularly unpopular decisions are made. *The intercept is not an explanation for the between-unit variance or the variance over time.* The intercept is simply a characterization of the variance that attempts to minimize the bias in the "true" explanation. The intercept is thus what Maddala (1977) calls "specific ignorance," in contrast to our general ignorance, which is captured in the error ($u_{nt}$).

## Estimating the LSDV Model[A]

When the intercept reflects variance from the cross-sections and the time series, the dummy variable model is not the only model appropriate to estimate the effects, but it is a relatively simple one. The dummy variable model replaces the estimate of the b's for the full pool with coefficients from the dummy variables. We incorporate a dummy variable by returning to the model in equation 3.1 and rewriting as follows:

$$Y_{nt} = \alpha_{nt} + x_{nt} \beta_k + u_{nt} \qquad [4.1]$$

where

$$u_{nt} = \lambda_t + \mu_n + \xi_{nt}$$

Therefore:

$$Y_{nt} = \alpha_{nt} + \lambda_t + \mu_n + X_{nt} \beta_k + \xi_{nt} \qquad [4.2]$$

for $n = (1 \dots N)$ cross sections
and $t = (1 \quad T)$ time series.

The $\lambda_t$ and $m_n$ are assumed to be "fixed" conditionally in the intercept while $\xi_{nt}$ is assumed to be random. The LSDV model should be used with some caution as it could be less efficient than other estimators and information could be lost when the $X$ vector contains time invariant variables.[11]

Earlier in this discussion, it was claimed that the difference between fixed or random effects was not worth pursuing too vehemently, but when an intercept is introduced this issue must be given more scrutiny. It is only in special cases that there would be no difference between fixed or random effects. Recall that fixed effects can be treated as random effects that are conditional on the relationship between the dummy variables and the regressors in the $X$ vector. In the absence of any omitted variables, the dummy variable estimator is identical to the unconditional GLS estimator (Mundlak, 1978). If the fixed effects, however, are related to omitted variables and those omitted variables are correlated to regressors in the $X$ vector, the LSDV and GLS estimators are not identical. Some *ad hoc* techniques have been developed to manage this particular estimation problem, but they are not taken up in this monograph.[12]

In the two tables that follow, the LSDV model is estimated and compared with the OLS model for two different data sets. The first

TABLE 4.1

OLS and LSDV Estimates for the Regression of Presidential
Popularity on Prior Approval

| | OLS<br>b<br>(standard error) | LSDV<br>b<br>(standard error) |
|---|---|---|
| CONSTANT | .0549<br>(.0197) | — |
| PRIOR | .8762 | .6003 |
| APPROVAL | (.0357) | (.0534) |
| UNIT EFFECTS | — | |
| 1954 | | .3001 (.0773) |
| 1958 | | .2008 (.0734) |
| 1959 | | .2937 (.0765) |
| 1960 | | .2647 (.0759) |
| 1962 | | .3436 (.0790) |
| 1965 | | .3028 (.0778) |
| 1966 | | .1067 (.0716) |
| 1967 | | .0199 (.0701) |
| 1969 | | .3134 (.0783) |
| 1970 | | .2048 (.0739) |
| 1973 | | −.1563 (.0706) |
| 1974 | | −.2678 (.0787) |
| 1978 | | .0812 (.0704) |
| 1979 | | −.1320 (.0736) |
| 1981 | | .2091 (.0747) |
| 1982 | | .0344 (.0701) |
| 1983 | | .0038 (.0701) |
| 1984 | | .1640 (.0720) |
| adj. $R^2$ | .736 | .768 |

data set is 144 cases ($n=6$, $t=24$) on the diplomatic climate (hostility
or friendliness) between an actor and a target. The contaminant influences on the variance in these data emanate from the cross-sections.
The second data set is on presidential popularity ($n$-18, $t=12$) where
the contaminant influences emanate from the cross-sections, which in
this data set are years in which the polls were taken. Remember that
because the cross-section is a year, the years do not have to be contiguous in time for the pooling design to be applied. The LSDV model
ferrets out and corrects for unique effects in time, not serial correlation or dependence through time. Table 4.1 compares OLS and LSDV
estimates for the effect of prior approval of the job the president is

TABLE 4.2

OLS and LSDV Estimates for the Regression of Diplomatic
Friendliness on Trade

| | OLS<br>b<br>(standard error) | LSDV<br>b<br>(standard error) |
|---|---|---|
| CONSTANT | 2.4764<br>(.2067) | — |
| TRADE | 4.0546<br>(.4137) | 1.0029<br>(.6326) |
| UNIT EFFECTS | — | |
| US | | 4.3262 (.4676) |
| CANADA | | 2.6976 (.2480) |
| UK | | 4.4556 (.3428) |
| FRANCE | | 4.7342 (.4405) |
| ITALY | | 4.3756 (.3992) |
| JAPAN | | 2.3932 (.2264) |
| adj. $R^2$ | .399 | .548 |
| pooled<br>Durbin-Watson<br>d | 1.23 | 1.64 |

doing with current levels of popularity while Table 4.2 compares estimates for the effect of trade on diplomatic friendliness.

Each cross-section, which in Table 4.2 represents an actor and a target of diplomatic activity, has a separate unit effect for the regression. These unit effects are listed as country names. Diplomatic activity is a continuous variable, which ranges from hostility to friendliness where positive values are friendly and negative values are hostile.[13] The unique contribution of each cross-section is given in this table in the b's. Please note that after unit effects are included, the pooled Durbin-Watson statistic increases from 1.23 to 1.64 which is still indicative of some contamination.

Another example is given in Table 4.1. This table compares OLS and LSDV estimates for the presidential popularity data, and so the unit in this example is the year. The inclusion of a lagged endogenous variable in the popularity regression prevents the Durbin-Watson d from being useful, and the appropriate Durbin h is not more revealing than the autocorrelation function. Over the 18 years of this data set, the unit effects remain positive except in three instances, two pertaining most likely to the OPEC oil embargo (1973, 1974) and the third most likely to the Iran Hostage Crisis under Carter (1979). There are other valleys, which, while still positive, remain as lower than average levels of popularity, for example 1967 (Vietnam prior to Tet).

The LSDV model clearly gives more information about particular influences from the cross-sections, and, in the two examples given here, better fits for the regression were obtained from the LSDV model as reflected in the adjusted $R^2$. The inclusion of unit effects deflates the effect of other variables in the $X$ vector as is seen in smaller coefficients for the right hand side variables.

Stimson (1985) correctly observes that the appropriateness of OLS depends upon the homogeneity of the cross-sections on the dependent variable. While specific tests for homogeneity can be made, they cannot be made within the confines of OLS. If we assume that in the OLS environment, homogeniety is likely to be a problem, then every effort should be made to establish the robustness of the coefficients. Robustness is the degree to which an estimate does not change by the introduction of new cases and time points, or by the omission of particular cases and time points. When new cases are introduced, as long as the sample distribution remains normal and the relationship between the $Y$ and $X$ variables remains linear, the estimates will retain robustness. Robustness is taken up in detail in Chapter 7, but it is worth mentioning in passing here because estimates are contaminated from many sources, including the heterogeneity of the pool.[14] As always, the residuals are an invaluable source of any information we might hope to utilize to gain efficiency under OLS.

# 5. THE RANDOM COEFFICIENT MODEL[B]

When the coefficients $\lambda_t$ *or* $\mu_n$ in equation 4.1 are not fixed in the regression intercept but rather are allowed to vary over time and space in a random manner, we then assume that the variables represented by these coefficients have a mean expectation of zero and are distributed with variance $\sigma^2$ under the conditions that $E[\mu_i \mu_j] = 0$ and $E[\lambda_t \lambda_s] = 0$ for $i \neq j$ and $t \neq s$. Moreover, $\lambda_t$, $\mu_n$, and $\xi_{nt}$ are uncorrelated. The error components model is often called the *random coefficient model* because this model utilizes the information contained in the covariance structure to derive unbiased and efficient estimates for the pooled time series. The random coefficient model utilizes random error in time, random error in space, and random error not unique to time or space but still random to the regression model to derive efficient and unbiased estimates. Error systematic to space (cross-section), error systematic to time, and error systematic to both are the components of total error in the random coefficient model. The obvious advantage of this model is that it does not require any assumptions about where the variance should be fixed, so, in the presence of weak or nonexistent theoretical justification, no incorrect assumptions need be made. The obvious disadvantage is that this model is driven by random error and so the error must be modeled accurately. Diagnostics are essential, and, with large data sets, correction via the variance-covariance matrix can become rather cumbersome. Moreover, there is no guarantee that the size of the effects will increase from the LSDV estimates. Error components is more efficient but in practical terms this may not lead to better, i.e., stronger and more statistically significant estimates. Part of the reason for this seeming paradox is that the random coefficient model requires better specified theory than the OLS or LSDV models. Theoretical effects may remain strong under random coefficient specification, but the general fit of the model may decline considerably. Moreover, omitted variables, multicollinearity, etc., will produce meaningless estimates under OLS, LSDV, or GLS assumptions, but they are harder to uncover in GLS. For this reason, it is usually worthwhile to begin with the simplest model first (e.g., OLS) if only to retain a benchmark of the magnitude and direction of the estimates. If the random coefficient model is the chosen course, then uncovering the influence of random error through time, across space, and elsewhere can be accomplished within the least squares framework as long as the empirical model does not violate standard least squares assumptions. Otherwise, maximum likelihood techniques might be necessitated.

## Estimating the Random Coefficient Model: GLS[B]

We would like to combine the systematic effects of space and time (systematic but not fixed), as well as any effects not systematic to space and time, in one slope coefficient for parsimony. To do this, we select a GLS estimator. The GLS estimator is as follows:

$$\beta = (X'\varphi^{-1}X)^{-1}X'\varphi^{-1}Y. \qquad [5.1]$$

Given

$$Y = X_{nt}\,\beta_k + u_{nt} \qquad [5.2]$$

where

$$u_{nt} = \lambda_t + \mu_n + \xi_{nt}$$

and

$\lambda_t$ are random over time and distributed $N\,(0, \sigma^2_\lambda \varphi)$

$\mu_n$ are random over cross sections and distributed $N\,(0, \sigma^2_\mu \psi)$

and

$\xi_{nt}$ are random over space and time and distributed $N\,(0, \sigma^2_\lambda \sigma^2_\nu \psi)$.

At this point, we do not assume $\lambda_t = \rho \lambda_{t-1} + v_t$ and $\sigma^2_\lambda = \rho^2_\nu / 1 - \rho^2$.[15] This is an ARMA variation of the GLS model we take up in the next section.

The joint distribution now looks like:

$$\varphi_{ii} = \sigma^2_\lambda + \sigma^2_\mu + \sigma^2_\nu$$

and the covariance between disturbances for two different cross-sections is:

$$\varphi_{ij} = \sigma^2_\lambda.$$

Note here that the cross-sectional variance is captured by the autoregression parameter in the error components model. This is the essential meaning behind the relationship between $\psi^{-1}$ and $\varphi$.

$$(P'P) = \begin{matrix} 1 & \rho_i & \rho^2_i & \rho^{t-1}_i & & \cdots \\ \rho_i & 1 & & & & \\ \rho^2_i & & 1 & & & \\ \cdot & & & 1 & & \\ \cdot & & & & 1 & \\ \rho^{t-1}_{2\,i} & o^{t-2}_i & & & & 1 \end{matrix}$$

$$= \sigma^2_\nu \varphi \quad \cdots$$

To estimate this model, modify equation 3.1 in the following way

$$Y^{**} = X^{**}_{nt}\beta_k + u^{**}_{nt}. \qquad [5.3]$$

where

$$Y^{**} = Y_{nt} - (1 - \sigma_u/\sigma_1)Y^*_n - (1 - \sigma_u/\sigma_2)Y^*_t \qquad [5.4]$$
$$+ ((1 - \sigma_u/\sigma_1) + (1 - \sigma_u/\sigma_2) + (1 - \sigma_u/\sigma_3))Y^*_{nt.}$$

$$X^{**} = X_{nt} - (1 - \sigma_u/\sigma_1)X^*_n - (1 - \sigma_u/\sigma_2)X^*_t \qquad [5.5]$$
$$+ ((1 - \sigma_u/\sigma_1) + (1 - \sigma_u/\sigma_2) + (1 - \sigma_u/\sigma_3))X^*_{nt.}$$

Define:

$$\sigma_1 = \sqrt{(\sigma^2_u + T\sigma^2_\mu)}$$
$$\sigma_2 = \sqrt{(\sigma^2_u + N\sigma^2_\lambda)}$$
$$\sigma_3 = \sqrt{(\sigma^2_u + T\sigma^2_\mu + N\sigma^2_\lambda)}$$

$\sigma_u = \sqrt{(\sigma^2_u)}$ generated by OLS
and $X^*_n = \text{mean}(X_n)$; $X^*_t = \text{mean}(X_t)$.

which are estimated from:

$$Y^*_n = \alpha_{nt} + \mu_n + X_{nt}\beta_k + \xi/T. \qquad [5.6]$$

$$Y^*_t = \alpha_{nt} + \lambda_t + X_{nt}\beta_k + \xi/N. \qquad [5.7]$$

$$Y^*_{nt} = \alpha_{nt} + X_{nt}\beta_k + \xi/NT. \qquad [5.8]$$

The estimator $\beta$ in equation 5.3 is an Estimated Generalized Least Squares (EGLS) estimator rather than an Exact GLS estimator because we have used estimates from prior regressions to establish the variance. In particular, the $\sigma^2 u$ is derived from OLS estimates in the first stage of estimation. Table 5.1 compares the OLS, LSDV, and GLS estimates for the presidential popularity data.

No ARMA process is assumed in this model and what Table 5.1 reveals is a relatively robust effect from prior approval across the three models. As anticipated, the GLS technique decreases general fit for the regression model. Because these models are so widely used, let us examine a second example from our time series data on diplomatic friendliness. In this model, no ARMA process is assumed, and so the random variation captured in the error components should reflect the heteroscedasticity of the pool. The random coefficient estimates are compared to the OLS and LSDV estimates in Table 5.2.

Table 5.2 gives the GLS estimates for the effect of trade on diplomatic friendliness. Comparison with the OLS and LSDV models reveals that again, the GLS fit is not as good as the OLS and LSDV fits,

TABLE 5.1
OLS, LSDV, and GLS Estimates for the Regression of Presidential
Popularity on Prior Approval

| | OLS b (standard error) | LSDV b (standard error) | GLS b (standard error) |
|---|---|---|---|
| CONSTANT | .0549 (.0197) | — | .0998 (.0416) |
| PRIOR APPROVAL | .8762 (.0357) | .6003 (.0534) | .6945 (.0474) |
| UNIT EFFECTS | — | | |
| 1954 | | .3001 (.0773) | |
| 1958 | | .2008 (.0773) | |
| 1959 | | .2937 (.0765) | |
| 1960 | | .2647 (.0759) | |
| 1962 | | .3436 (.0790) | |
| 1965 | | .3028 (.0778) | |
| 1966 | | .1067 (.0716) | |
| 1967 | | .0199 (.0701) | |
| 1969 | | .3134 (.0783) | |
| 1970 | | .2048 (.0739) | |
| 1973 | | −.1563 (.0706) | |
| 1974 | | −.2678 (.0787) | |
| 1978 | | .0812 (.0704) | |
| 1979 | | −.1320 (.0736) | |
| 1981 | | .2091 (.0747) | |
| 1982 | | .0344 (.0701) | |
| 1983 | | .0038 (.0701) | |
| 1984 | | .1640 (.0720) | |
| adj. $R^2$ | .736 | .768 | .499 |

but the specific effects are much more likely to be reliable. The difference in effect (from $b = 4.05$ in OLS to $b = 1.0$ in LSDV) is startling, but the GLS estimate of the effect ($b = 1.35$) is closer to the LSDV effect and is, moreover, unbiased and efficient.

## An ARMA Variation of the GLS Model[B]

From examination of the autocorrelation function (ACF) and partial autocorrelation function (PACF) from the regression on presidential popularity, the assumption of a first-order autoregressive process is warranted. These functions represent the correlation between the regression residuals at one time point and the regression residuals at a

TABLE 5.2

OLS, LSDV, and GLS Estimates for the Regression of Diplomatic
Friendliness on Trade

| | OLS<br>b<br>(standard error) | LSDV<br>b<br>(standard error) | GLS<br>b<br>(standard error) |
|---|---|---|---|
| CONSTANT | 2.4764<br>(.2067 | — | 3.6743<br>(.4910) |
| TRADE | 4.0546<br>(.4137) | 1.0029<br>(.6326) | 1.3547<br>(.6067) |
| UNIT EFFECTS | — | | |
| US | | 4.3262 (.4676) | |
| CANADA | | 2.6976 (.2480) | |
| UK | | 4.4556 (.3428) | |
| FRANCE | | 4.7342 (.4405) | |
| ITALY | | 4.3756 (.3992) | |
| JAPAN | | 2.3932 (.2264) | |
| adj. $R^2$<br>pooled | .399 | .548 | .027 |
| Durbin-Watson<br>d | 1.23 | 1.64 | |

previous time point. They are re-created in Figure 5.1. The clear
decay in the ACF and the single significant spike in the PACF are indicative of a first-order autoregressive process. The ACF (autocorrelation function) is the simple bivariate correlation between two time
points where the PACF (partial autocorrelation function) is the correlation controlling for the influence of other significant lag effects.
The PACF is used to detect the influence of later lags holding early
lags constant or vice versa. If more than one spike is significant in the
PACF, it is indicative of other lag effects. In Figure 5.1, there is only
one significant spike in the PACF reflecting a one-period lag effect
and the standard AR(1) process of autoregression in the residuals.

The simple ARMA variation of the EGLS model assumes an autoregressive process is driving the variance. Assuming a first-order
ARMA process for equation 3.1, write:

$$Y_{nt} = X_{nt}\beta_k + e_{nt} \qquad [5.9]$$

where $e_{nt} = \mu_n + \lambda_t + \xi_{nt}$.

Now assume $\lambda_t$ is distributed $N(0, \sigma^2_\lambda \Psi)$ and $\lambda_t = \rho\lambda_{t-1} + v_t$.

| AUTOCORRELATION FUNCTION | | LAG | PARTIAL AUTOCORRELATION FUNCTION | |
|---|---|:---:|---|---|
| 0 | +1 | | 0 | +1 |
| ************** | | 1 | ************** |
| ************* | | 2 | * |
| ************ | | 3 | * |
| ********** | | 4 | * |
| ********** | | 5 | * |
| ********* | | 6 | |
| ******** | | 7 | |
| ******** | | 8 | |
| ******** | | 9 | |
| ******* | | 10 | * |
| ****** | | 11 | * |
| ****** | | 12 | * |
| ***** | | 13 | |
| ***** | | 14 | |
| **** | | 15 | * |

**Figure 5.1: Residuals for Regression of Presidential Popularity on Prior Approval**

$$\sigma^2_\lambda = \sigma^2_\nu / (1 - \rho^2).^{16}$$

The reestimated ARMA-GLS model is given in Table 5.3 with comparison estimates from the GLS estimation reported in Table 5.2 for the presidential popularity data.

The results in Table 5.3 compare two ARMA models (OLS and Pooled GLS) with the GLS results without the ARMA assumption. Only the pooled ARMA estimate recognizes the contribution of each cross-section to the variance. The ARMA assumption strengthens the coefficients in the OLS model ($b = .9097$), but the unbiased GLS estimate is about one-third of that ($b = .3115$) for the effect of prior approval on presidential popularity. The precise contributions of each of the cross-sections, in this case years in which the poll was taken, is unknown. While the ARMA model corrects for nonconstant variance and the estimates of the effects improve, the general fit of the model deteriorates. The trade-off is one of efficiency and unbiasedness in the estimate for the overall fit. A model, however, that tends to outperform GLS and ARMA-GLS is based on recognition of the contribution of cross-sections and the first-order autoregression. This is accomplished via seemingly unrelated regression.

TABLE 5.3
ARMA Estimation of Presidential Popularity on Prior Approval

|  | GLS b (standard error) | OLS-ARMA b (standard error) | POOLED GLS-ARMA b (standard error) |
|---|---|---|---|
| CONSTANT | .0998 (.0419) | .0280 (.0141) | .2300 (.0506) |
| PRIOR APPROVAL | .6945 (.0474) | .9097 (.0312) | .3115 (.0633) |
| adj. $R^2$ | .499 | .795 | .128 |

for all ARMA models reported above, $\rho$ = .917 for first order transfer function and $\delta$ = .0001.

## A Seemingly Unrelated Regression Version of the GLS Model [B]

When the slope coefficients in the model:

$$Y_{nt} = \alpha_{nt} + X_{nt}\beta_k + e_{nt} \qquad [5.10]$$

vary over the cross-sections alone, the relationship of the variable $Y_{nt}$ to the variable $X_{nt}$ is different for each cross-section, but remains constant for each time series within the cross-section. We have already utilized a dummy variable model to adjust for the unique variation in each cross-section, but there is a more efficient way to estimate a pooled regression under these conditions. This method permits us to correct for a first-order autoregressive process as well. This method treats each cross-section and the time series within that cross-section as a separate equation that is unrelated to any other cross-section (and time series within the cross section) in the pooled data set. This approach was first developed by Zellner (1962) as a way to manage systems of equations and is referred to as Seemingly Unrelated Regression.

The SUR estimator is a modified EGLS estimator of the following form:

$$\beta = (X'_{nt}\Sigma^{-1}X_{nt})^{-1}X'_{nt}\Sigma^{-1}Y_{nt} \qquad [5.11]$$

and
$\Sigma$ has elements $\sigma_{nt} = T^{-1}e_ie_j$
where $i,j = (1, 2 \ldots N)$ cross-sections

and $T = (1 \ldots T)$ time series.

The SUR estimator is biased if the number of explanatory variables in each cross-section is different, but it is still consistent and more efficient than applying OLS to each cross-section separately. For a pooled regression with an SUR estimator, the researcher must make sure that no stepwise techniques are used and also that each cross-section retains the same exact specification of exogenous effects in the $X$ vector.[17]

In the presence of first-order autoregressive disturbances, the estimation of $\beta$ in 5.11 requires an additional assumption:

$$\beta^* = (X^{*'}\Sigma^{-1}X^*)^{-1}X^{*'}\Sigma^{-1}Y^* \qquad [5.12]$$

where

$$X^* = PX \,; X^*_{it} = X_{it} - \rho x_{it-1} \text{ and}$$

$$Y^*_{it} = PY \,; Y_{it} = Y_{it} - \rho y_{it-1}.$$

The estimated covariance is derived from the transformed least squares estimates:

$$U^*_{nt} = Y^*_{nt} - X^*_{nt}\beta^*_k. \qquad [5.13]$$

Table 5.4 compares EGLS-ARMA and SUR-EGLS-ARMA estimates for a first-order autoregressive process in the diplomatic friendliness data.

Consider the increase in the strength of the coefficient for trade in the EGLS-SUR-ARMA version of this model. The coefficient for trade ($b = 2.3705$) increases from $b = 1.3547$ even in the simple EGLS model. The general fit of the model improves as well from adjusted $R^2 = .027$ $to$ $R^2 = .590$. When the SUR version is incorporated, the fit declines, but only slightly, from $R^2 = .590$ $to$ $R^2 = .470$, but the coefficient for trade increases from $b = 2.3705$ to $b = 3.4648$. SUR takes a separate rho estimate for each cross-section to fit the ARMA parameter in the estimation of the linear model. The diagnostic information needed to derive these separate rho estimates can be gained by independent estimation of each cross-section or by unique estimation of the variance for each cross-section under a pooled OLS or GLS model. In the estimation reported in Table 5.4, six different estimates of rho were derived by taking the ratio of the OLS residual variance to the combined OLS and LSDV residual variance. Under conditions of heterogeneity, the SUR estimation can prove invaluable because it

TABLE 5.4
SUR Estimation of Diplomatic Friendliness on Trade

|  | GLS<br>b<br>(standard error) | GLS-ARMA<br>b<br>(standard error) | GLS-SUR-ARMA<br>b<br>(standard error) |
|---|---|---|---|
| CONSTANT | 3.6743<br>(.4960) | 8.8115<br>(2.3724) | 2.8306<br>(.2055) |
| TRADE | 1.3547<br>(.6067) | 2.3705<br>(.4067) | 3.4648<br>(.3630) |
| adj. $R^2$ | .027 | .590 | .470 |

is much more sensitive to individual contributions. The SUR model is actually a special case of a more general model that permits the parameters to vary randomly over the cross-sections. This model is taken up in more detail in the next section.

## The Swamy Random Coefficient Model[B]

When the coefficients in the regression equation are not fixed but allowed to vary randomly over the cross-sections in the pool, we characterize the resulting model as a random coefficient model, which was developed by Swamy (1970). In this model, there are two estimators, $\beta$ and $\beta_\iota$. $\beta$ represents the mean of a probability distribution from which an individual $\beta_i$ in the pool is drawn. Our task is to determine the mean $\beta$ from which we can estimate individual cross-section effects $\beta_i$. This model is as follows:

$$Y_{it} = X_{it}(\beta + \mu_i) + e_{it}; \text{ for } i = (1 \ldots N) \text{ and } t = (1 \ldots T). \quad [5.14]$$

We assume no serial correlation in this version of the model because it complicates the covariance matrix, and, while it is theoretically manageable, in application serial correlation it is somewhat intractable. The regression equation in 5.14 is a model that corrects for heteroscedastic error by assuming constant variance within the cross-section. The advantage of using the random coefficient model over the fixed SUR model is that we are able to predict to classes of subgroups (cross-sections) and are able to predict values of the dependent variable given a particular subgroup. This model treats the pool as a set of *repeated* samples, and so, intuitively it makes sense to find a mean estimate then try to predict individual subsamples (cross-sections) given the mean value and an assumption about the distribution of the pool.

Of course, if the pool is not well represented by a normal distributional assumption, other distributions can be substituted, but the attractive properties of least squares estimation do not necessarily follow. The Swamy model, like any random coefficient model, attempts to assess the proportion of residual variance explained by the addition of a random parameter. This proportion depends directly on the variance of the residual vector and the variance of the added parameter. Needless to say, comparability and homogeneity will assist in making the variance more amenable to the EGLS-Swamy model. The Swamy model takes the following form:

$$Y_{nt} = Y_{nt} \beta + Z\mu + e_{nt}. \qquad [5.15]$$

The covariance is given by $\xi = QQ'$ *where* $Q = (Z\mu + e_{nt})$.

$$\beta = (X'\Phi^{-1}X)^{-1}X'\Phi^{-1}Y \qquad [5.16]$$

which is only the weighted average of the least squares estimators for individual cross-sections. In the absence of serial correlation, this model is advantageous because, no matter how long the time series, the determination of the mean estimator is dependent solely on the number of exogenous effects, i.e., the size of the $X$ vector. Judge et al. (1985) describe the GLS-Swamy estimator as the weighted average of a "between estimator" and a "within estimator." This model permits us to distinguish between variance that arises from within the cross-section and variance that arises from the differences between the cross-sections. To illustrate the Swamy coefficient model, we use data from diplomatic friendliness. Table 5.5 compares Swamy estimates for the regression of diplomatic friendliness on trade.

The Swamy coefficients in Table 5.5 include a lagged endogenous variable for diplomatic friendliness. There are three Swamy estimates: a pooled OLS estimate, a Swamy-GLS estimate, and a Swamy-GLS-ARMA estimate. Instead of what essentially becomes a "fixing" the rho for each cross-section, the actual residual output is used from each cross-section to weight the contribution of that cross-section. In the ARMA version of this model, the weighted $x$ and $y$ vectors are assumed to follow a first-order autoregressive process. The ARMA

TABLE 5.5
Swamy Estimation of Diplomatic Friendliness on Trade

|  | POOLED OLS b (standard error) | GLS b (standard error) | GLS-ARMA b (standard error) |
|---|---|---|---|
| CONSTANT | 2.9582 (.2351) | 3.0100 (.5360) | 1.4858 (.2827) |
| FRIEND (t-1) | .0267 (.0049) | .2119 (.0720) | .6531 (.0572) |
| TRADE | 3.2271 (.0424) | 3.3380 (1.3654) | 5.2364 (.4575) |
| adj. $R^2$ | .212 | .064 | .603 |
| $\rho$ |  | .478 |  |
| $\delta$ |  | .9610 | .0005 |
| $\phi$ |  |  | .03 |
| $\theta$ |  |  | 4.5 |

model reported in Table 5.5 has an estimated rho for the entire pool, not an estimated rho for individual cross-sections. The effect of trade on diplomatic friendliness is quite stable for both the Swamy versions of the OLS and GLS models, but the effect is even stronger in the GLS-ARMA version. The general fit improves in the ARMA version as does the influence of the lagged endogenous variable.

The advantage of the Swamy model over the SUR version is again in unbiasedness and efficiency of the estimated parameters, but the strength of the coefficients and the general fit may deteriorate. Swamy coefficients can be considered as *pooled weighted least squares* coefficients and can be cumbersome to estimate in large pools. The independence in the error, i.e., the independence between the error from cross-sectional variation and the error from time serial variation is assumed here but may still be contaminating the coefficients. The robustness of the coefficients is called into question when the assumption of independence is violated. In the Swamy model we correct first for the cross-sectional contribution to contamination and then reestimate via ARMA to correct for autoregression. There is no evidence that this two-stage estimate is unbiased or efficient. It is much better to treat these problems together in one estimator, and essentially this is what the Hsaio estimator tries to do.

## The Hsiao Random Coefficient Model[B]

A natural extension of the Swamy model is the Hsiao (1975) model. The Hsaio model employs a mean estimator for the cross-sections, but also includes a mean estimator for the time series. The model takes the following form:

$$Y_{nt} = x_{nt} \beta_k + Z \mu_n + Z \lambda_t + e_{nt.} \qquad [5.17]$$

The new covariance incorporates effects from time and from the cross-sections:
$\Phi = WW'$ where $W = (Z\mu_n + Z\lambda_t + e_{nt})$.
The estimator is similar to the Swamy estimator:

$$\beta = (X'\Phi^{-1}X)^{-1}X'\Phi^{-1}Y \qquad [5.18]$$

but the estimator is not as straightforward. This model requires a fairly large $N$ and $T$, and so, when the effects of serial correlation are included, there is no simple transformation matrix for the pool. In addition, the variances for the parameters $\mu_n$ and $\lambda_t$ are very often not known and must be estimated from the sample. The Hildreth-Houck estimation technique is time-consuming and expensive as residual variance must be estimated for each time series and each cross-section individually. An alternative is to exclude the random parameter $\lambda_t$ from the model and attempt to include time effects as fixed (in an intercept term). Then, estimate the joint covariance from the interaction of the fixed effects with the error.

It is rather unlikely that any pooled regression problem will remain intractable because of the difficulties imposed by the Hsaio model. Indeed, some of the most difficult problems do not emanate from attempts to gain efficiency or decrease bias but rather from estimation under an incorrect assumption. Nonlinearity in the dependent variable, for example, or unstable time series (nonstationarity) are special problems in a pool.[18] The random coefficient model is particularly attractive as a pooled regression model when the time effects are not very stable. Stability is threatened when the mean is fixed but not known or the slope coefficients are stochastic but not stationary. Compare the Hsiao estimates in Table 5.6 below for diplomatic friendliness.

Table 5.6 shows both pooled SUR Hsiao estimates and Hsaio-GLS estimates for the effect of trade on diplomatic friendliness. The lagged endogenous variable is also included in this regression. The

TABLE 5.6
Hsaio Estimation of Diplomatic Friendliness on Trade

|  | OLS b (standard error) | GLS b (standard error) |
|---|---|---|
| CONSTANT | 1.7299 (.3021) | 3.558 (.5440) |
| FRIEND (t-1) | 1.3282 (.1567) | .2727 (.1083) |
| TRADE | 6.4699 (.9126) | 3.0938 (1.8011) |
| adj. $R^2$ | .353 | .037 |
| $\rho$ |  |  |
| US |  | .6418 |
| CAN |  | .5498 |
| UK |  | .4172 |
| FRANCE |  | .5155 |
| ITALY |  | .4765 |
| JAPAN |  | .5037 |

Hsaio model differs only slightly from the Swamy model in that independent $\rho$'s are assigned to each cross-section in the GLS version. The pooled SUR version relies on one $\rho$ to estimate autoregression for the pool. The fit of the GLS version is unattractive, but fit is traded for unbiasedness and efficiency. The effect of trade is inflated a bit in the Hsaio OLS model as compared with the more efficient GLS model. The lagged variable is also inflated under OLS assumptions. Again, it is worth noting that Hsaio estimates can be cumbersome to obtain if the pool is comprised of a large number of cross-sections. Compared to the Swamy estimates, the Hsaio estimates are more efficient and less biased. What might appear perplexing is the sensitivity of the fit parameter ($R^2$) to the different models. Each model relies on unique transformations of the residual variance and, thus, $R^2$ is not, strictly speaking, comparable across the different models. Since $R^2$ is the square of the multiple correlation coefficient, the GLS $R^2$ becomes particularly sensitive to $\rho$'s influence, i.e., the strength of the autoregressive process in the regression. Diagnostics on the partial autocorrelation function (PACF) and ACF are helpful in establishing the robustness of these coefficients under alternative AR assumptions. Robustness is easily lost to nonlinearity, and, in that case, the linearity assumptions of least squares might undermine the utility of least squares estimation. An attractive alternative to nonlinear estimation is a recasting of the theoretical problem into a nonlinear form, then estimating this new form without the linearity assumption, e.g., via maximum likelihood. Yet, a simpler way and one that permits retention of the least squares framework is achieved in the switching model.

## The Switching Model[B]

One of the simpler but more elegant regression models that is particularly valuable in the presence of a nonlinear function is the switching model. This class of models originated from electrical engineering where discrete functions were needed to explain unique and unrelated processes. In the social and behavioral sciences, the switching model has been utilized to explain social choices, and one of the more widely used applications of the switching models is to the choice of joining a union.

The utility of the switching model to pooled regression becomes obvious when its simplicity is added to its elegance. The central idea is that there is some underlying process that works for some of the cross-sections in the pool and another process at work for other cross-sections. This approach is attractive because pooled time series are so often a concatenation of processes frequently unobservable and seen only in the variance of the cross-sections. The switching model allows unique assumptions about these processes to be made *at the theoretical level* rather than at the empirical level. Estimation then follows directly from the theoretical specification.

The estimation of the switching model relies on fitting *pieces* of the regression equation, which represent or approximate changes in parametric values from one process of interest to another. These values can change as a function of time or a function of other variables or groups of variables (omitted or included in the regression model). The shifts in the slope coefficients or pieces of the regression model are called *regimes*. When the regimes are influenced by unobserved processes and variables not captured in the regression model, the switching model can quickly become problematic to estimate. Too many assumptions about the omitted effects may make estimation intractable. When the processes are known and the theoretical model well specified, however, the switching model is both attractive and simple to estimate. A switching model for a pooled time series might assume the following structure:

$$Y_{nt} = X_{nt}\,\beta_k + u_{nt} \qquad\qquad [5.19]$$

where $\beta_k = \beta + \delta_t$
and if $\delta_t < t_n$ , $\beta_{kt} = \beta_1$
    if $\delta_t > t_n$ , $\beta_{kt} = \beta_2$.

In this model, the two regimes are not "joined," but an additional assumption could be made to join the two regimes.
Assume:

$$X'\,(\beta_1 - \beta_2) = 0. \qquad\qquad [5.20]$$

It should be noted that the regimes in equation 5.19 are *determined* in the sense that the parametric values are fixed at $\beta_1\ or\ \beta_2$, but these values could be stochastic as the following assumption illustrates:

$$\beta_{kt} = \delta_t\,\beta_k + v_{t.} \qquad\qquad [5.21]$$

The advantage of the switching model is that more difficult extensions in functional form, for example, extensions to cubic or quadratic polynomials are still easily accommodated within the least squares framework.[19] Let us compare two switching models—one with a non-stochastic assumption and one with a stochastic assumption—from our presidential popularity data. Assume that a unique process determines why the public approves of what the president is doing at any given time and another process governs why the public disapproves. For example, disapproval might be driven by the pocketbook while approval might be driven by ideology. Table 5.7 shows the results from two pooled regressions of a switching model. The first model assumes that the regimes are governed by a fixed process while the second model assumes that the process is stochastic.

Table 5.7 gives the exact form of the switching assumption, which for the non-stochastic version amounts to a simple dummy variable model, but for the stochastic version includes an interaction effect. The dependent variable is the percent polled who approve of what the president is doing in any given month throughout the sample years in the pool. The results of estimation under OLS assumptions show that there is very little difference between the two models in terms of the

TABLE 5.7
Switching Model Estimates for the Regression of Presidential
Popularity on Prior Approval

| | Non-Stochastic $(bX_{nt} + d)$ (standard error) | Stochastic $(b + d)X_{nt}$ (standard error) |
|---|---|---|
| CONSTANT | 42.1502 (.6254) | 44.1369 (.5148) |
| PRIOR APPROVAL | 13.2092 (.2117) | 12.0595 (1.0179) |
| SWITCH | 9.9607 (.2224) | |
| INTERACTION | — | 16.6154 (1.6566) |
| adj. $R^2$ | .992 | .832 |

general fit or the effect of prior approval. The non-stochastic assumption, i.e., a fixed parameter value, leads to a slightly weaker effect from the process variable than the stochastic assumption. This comparison could be interpreted to mean that the process of approving or disapproving is driven not only by a "switch" but also by the interaction of the switch with prior behavior, for example, the desire to remain consistent in one's view of the president may inhibit approvers from disapproving as frequently or as strongly as they might otherwise.

The switching model can be simply treated as a dummy variable model, but it is not equivalent to the LSDV model discussed earlier for two reasons. First, LSDV makes no claim about the processes that generate the variance, and second, LSDV specifies a linear functional form from which predicted behavior follows. The switching model by contrast permits all kinds of functional relationships to be assumed, including nonlinear ones. But more importantly, the switching model allows the processes that generate unique variances in the cross-sections to be modeled more directly. Under the switching model, groups of cross-sections can be clustered and analyzed for their group contributions to the variance.

# The ARCH Model[C]

A switching model can sometimes correct for underlying nonnormal disturbances, but very often, the nonnormality reflects a combination of mistaken assumptions. In the case of a pooled regression model where autoregression is conditional on the heteroscedasticity, a special class of models has been developed. This class of models is designed to specify a covariance structure that best represents the underlying heteroscedasticity. So far, we have been less concerned with the precise form of the heteroscedasticity, but it makes sense to try to better specify this source of contamination. There are a number of assumptions that can be made about the covariance structure when the errors are heteroscedastic. We consider a special case quite likely to arise in pooled regression, that is, when the autoregression is related to the heteroscedasticity: the Autoregressive Conditional Heteroscedasticity or ARCH model.

In a pooled regression, we often find it difficult to model a stochastic process in the time series without an assumption of homoscedastic disturbances. The ARCH model allows us to model a stochastic process under an assumption that the errors do not follow a homoscedastic structure. Up to now we have first corrected for the heteroscedasticity before we estimated the pooled regression model, but this two-step procedure assumes that the autoregression and the heteroscedasticity are unrelated. The estimates produced are inefficient. What we would like to do is to model time stochastically, conditional on the heteroscedasticity in the pool. Assume, for example, that the time series follows a first-order autoregressive process, but the residuals tend to cluster at particularly high or low values over the series. The autoregression may be more serious at high values or reflect a second-order process different from the first-order process observed at lower values. The time series residuals then are showing a nonconstant variance through time. We can say that the first-order assumption is conditional on some underlying heteroscedasticity in the pool.

In the ARCH model we are assuming that the disturbances are related or dependent on each other in some combination of ways. In the random coefficient models we have examined so far, we have assumed independence among the processes that might generate the variation in the time series from those processes that might generate the variation in the cross-sections. In the ARCH model, by contrast, we assume that the two processes are related in a way that expresses itself in the structure of the errors. When we model this structure, we identify a functional form for the errors and we frequently have a theoretical explanation as to why the error might follow a particular functional form [e.g., moving average and autoregressive) for one group of cross-sections, another functional form for a second set, and so on. We then condition the error structure within each cross-section on the functional form(s) specified for the cross-sections.

For example, the choice to approve might be related to prior approval because individuals want to appear consistent once they have made the commitment to approve. On the other hand, disapproval requires no such commitment, and, moreover, there is likely to be a population of "switchers" disapprovers who approved last time but are now disenchanted, or disapprovers who changed their approval consideration in the current period. In short, disapprovers might be less stable over time as a group, and the instability in the process could be manifest in any number of ways. The functional form of the switching process might be nonlinear, or, even if it is linear, it might be nonstationary. On the other hand, the autoregressive parameter might be very weak or nonexistent, given the lack of a clear relationship with prior approval. Diagnostics for each group process would again be highly valuable in determining the form of the AR process and the functional form of the switching regime.

In the ARCH model, the autoregressive process is dependent on the salience of the proximity of one error point to another. The structure of this linkage could easily extend beyond a first-order process unique to each group of cross-sections in the pool. In order to estimate an ARCH model, we need the conditional means and conditional variances of the dependent variable and the residuals. In essence, we are trying to model the error as a function of some intercept and a slope coefficient for the previous point in time, both of which are related to the value of the independent variables. In the very simple form of the ARCH model that follows, the independent variables are assumed to be normal with a mean of zero and a unit variance, but the form of the distribution depends on the quality of heteroscedasticity in the pool. We might wish, for example, to model the approval process as a truncated normal distribution. Taking the regular normal distributional assumption for the ARCH model would lead to conditional means and variances that look like:

$$E\left[u_t \mid u_{t-1}\right] = 0; \quad VAR\left[u_t \mid u_{t-1}\right] = \alpha_0 + \alpha_1 e^2_{t-1} \qquad [5.22]$$

$$E[y_t \mid y_{t-1}] = X_n'\beta; \quad VAR[y_t \mid y_{t-1}] = \alpha_0 + \alpha_1 e^2_{t-1} \qquad [5.23]$$

and

$$\sigma^2 = \alpha_0/(1 - \alpha_1).$$

An (asymptotically inefficient) estimator for $\alpha_0, \alpha_1$, and $\beta$ can be derived via least squares, although a more efficient estimator is derived via maximum likelihood techniques.

When the normal distribution is assumed for the heteroscedastic properties of the underlying processes being modeled, the ARCH model simplifies to a switching model or, even more simply, the LSDV model. The advantage of the more complicated ARCH model is that, should the LSDV model and its assumptions prove unworkable, the ARCH model offers an alternative. Instead of one process with effects of different magnitudes (LSDV), or one model with different magnitudes and directions (switching), there could be several processes with unique forms of the process, including magnitude and direction not necessarily linear.

## Conclusions on the Random Coefficient Model

The random coefficient model is quite flexible for pooled regression, and there is virtually no process that cannot be accommodated within its confines as long as there are no simultaneous processes occurring within the model, or there is no more than one equation to be estimated. When there are structural equations, simultaneous processes, and to a certain extent even lagged endogenous variables or more difficult nonlinear forms to be modeled, the random coefficient model must be adapted to reflect these violations in the assumptions to attain unbiased and efficient estimates. Yet there is no guarantee that the random coefficient model will outperform OLS or LSDV in the presence of violated assumptions, and the empirical reality may be quite the contrary, i.e., that OLS is more robust against violations than GLS. Nevertheless, there are times in the course of research when the violation must be addressed, and GLS seems incapable of managing the problem. This is particularly the case when there are multi-equation models, complex lag structures, or contaminating lag structures. In the next chapter, we look at some advanced topics of particular concern to pooled regression. Chapter 6 examines structural equation models and estimation via maximum likelihood techniques.

## 6. THE STRUCTURAL EQUATION MODEL[B]

So far, this monograph has focused on single-equation models using data from a pool of cross-sections and time series to estimate the various parameters in the model. Many problems in social and business science consist not of a single equation but of a *system of equations*. Although we frequently incorporate lagged endogenous variables into the vector of right-hand-side variables, their presence tends to complicate even single-equation modeling in a pooled regression structure. The inclusion of a lagged endogenous variable is a serious source of bias and, in many instances, may just prevent estimation entirely. Endogeneity violates the assumption of the linear model that variables on the right-hand-side are uncorrelated (orthogonal) to the error. Because an endogenous effect is correlated with the error in regression terms, the variance-covariance matrix is singular and unable to be inverted to derive an estimate of the effect of the exogenous variables on the dependent variable.[20] A simple but reliable approach to managing violations of orthogonality in the linear model is through two-stage estimation. The two-stage estimator relies on the use of a surrogate or *instrument* for those variables that violate orthogonality.

### Two-Stage Estimation[B]

Consider the following equations:

$$Y_1 = \alpha_1 + x_1\beta_1 + x_2\beta_2 + \gamma_2 Y_2 + u_1 \qquad [6.1]$$

$$Y_2 = \alpha_2 + x_2\beta_2 + x_3\beta_3 + \gamma_1 Y_1 + u_2. \qquad [6.2]$$

In order to develop a pooled estimator for this model, we have to first correct for the lack of orthogonality between the true exogenous effects in the right-hand-side vector and the endogenous effects that appear on the right-hand side. Intuitively, it makes sense to use a substitute for the endogenous effects in equation 6.1, a substitute that would be orthogonal to the right-hand-side variables. Indeed, this is how two-stage estimation works. First, an instrument is developed as a substitute for the endogenous variable. This instrument is then utilized to orthogonalize (derive a unique solution for) the effect of the right-hand-side variables on the left-hand side.

The value of this approach is that two-stage estimation can be accomplished within the least squares framework. The disadvantage of two-stage estimation is that the estimates are very sensitive to the size of the sample (Judge et al., 1985). It is also true that the two-stage estimator is still a biased estimator because the information contained in the covariance matrix has been ignored. The former problem may be slightly alleviated by the size of the pool, while the latter incorporates the information in the covariance matrix. The third stage is especially important for pooled regression if the structural equation models contain a lagged variable (endogenous or not).

## REDUCED FORM[B]

The central problem in simultaneous equation models is identification. Identification should ideally answer two questions of interest to the researcher. First, does this system of equations have a solution? Second, does this system have a *unique* solution? These two questions are answered by establishing the *rank* and the *order* of the system in its simplest or *reduced* form.[21] The reduced form equations recast the system into a set of variables and parameters that summarize important relationships of the system.

For our example in equation 6.1, the reduced form takes on the following structure:

$$Y \Gamma + X \beta = E \qquad [6.3]$$

$$Y = -XB \Gamma^{-1} + E \Gamma^{-1} \qquad [6.4]$$

and $\Gamma^{-1}$ is a matrix of parameters for the endogenous effects on the right-hand side of the equation in 6.1.

## INSTRUMENTAL LEAST SQUARES[B]

We now need to estimate $\Gamma^{-1}$ via an instrumental least squares technique. From the conflict data, we can generate an instrument in the first stage of estimation by running the following regression on the full pool:

$$Y*_1 = x_1\beta_1 + x_2\beta_2 + x_3\beta_3 + u_1 \qquad [6.5]$$

and then create a new variable from this OLS regression for the endogenous effect $Y_1$ in equation 6.1. This new variable is the instrument to use in the second stage in place of the old variable $Y_1$.

$$Y_2 = \alpha_2 + x_2\beta_2 + x_2\beta_2 + Y*_1 + u_2. \qquad [6.6]$$

It is of particular interest to consider this same problem, but include a *lagged* endogenous variable. We shall accomplish this by changing equation 6.1 in the following way:

$$Y_1 = \alpha_1 + x_1\beta_1 + x_2\beta_2 + \lambda_2 Y_{2(t-1)} + u_1. \qquad [6.7]$$

$Y_{2(t-1)}$ is a one period lag for the variable $Y_2$.

The inclusion of the lagged endogenous variable introduces autoregression into the error, and so we are now faced with the necessity of including the information in the variance-covariance matrix to correctly estimate the model. One approach that has been suggested by Malvinaud (1970) is to include the lagged exogenous variables as part of the instrument in the first stage, then in the second stage simply estimate the model like any other two-stage model. More formally, this approach would look like the following:

$$Y_{nt} = x_1\beta_1 + x_2\beta_2 + x_3\beta_3 + \gamma_1 Y_{nt}(t-1) + u_{nt}. \qquad [6.8]$$

The instrument is developed as follows:

$$Y^*_{n(t-1)} = x_1\beta_1 + x_1\beta_{1(t-1)} + x_2\beta_2 + x_2\beta_2(t-1) + x_3\beta_3 + x_3\beta_{3(t-1)} \quad [6.9]$$
$$+ u_{nt}.$$

Before we get too far ahead of ourselves, let us compare estimates from the two simultaneous equation models we have considered so far: one with and one without a lagged endogenous variable. This comparison is shown in Table 6.1.

Table 6.1 shows the results from two different regressions. The first regression estimates are two-stage OLS estimates for the effect of trade on diplomatic friendliness. While trade is directly related to diplomatic friendliness, trade itself is also related to openness, national product, the import/export structure, and world prices. Thus, in lieu of trade we use an instrument that in the second stage we can directly estimate in the regression for conflict.

The results show that the introduction of an instrument changes the direction of the intercept. This change can often arise because the instrument is developed from all the other right-hand-side variables in

TABLE 6.1

Two-Stage OLS Estimates for the Regression of Diplomatic
Friendliness on Trade

| | Lagged endogenous included b (standard error) | Lagged endogenous excluded b (standard error) |
|---|---|---|
| CONSTANT | −.4532* (.4931) | −.4119 (.5343) |
| INSTRUMENT FOR TRADE | 1.6172 (.2840 ) | 2.3578 (.2642) |
| FRIEND (t-1) | .3566 (.0702) | — |
| adj. $R^2$ pooled | .451 | .355 |
| Durbin-Watson d | — | 1.12 |

*Change in sign caused by inclusion of instrument where some of the variables in the instrument are negatively related to friendliness, in this case, real gross national product.

the two-equation model, and some of the effects may counter each other. In this example, real gross national product is the culprit so that, while overall imports and exports (trade) may have a positive effect on diplomatic friendliness, the national product (which may be an indicator of power and wealth) may have just the opposite effect. The instrument in this example appears relatively robust in the presence of the lag.

We run a similar set of regressions under assumptions appropriate to a random coefficient model (Swamy). These results are reported in Table 6.2.

The Swamy estimates are reported with and without the lag, with and without the assumption of an AR(1) process. In this example, the instrument is built from variables weighted by the residuals. The estimates for the instrument are very robust as is the estimate of the influence of the lag. The intercept is once again in a positive direction in the Swamy model and is statistically significant. The general fit cannot be meaningfully applied here to the $R^2$ statistic because the residual variance is used to improve the predictive power of the model. The independent effects, however, can be interpreted much like any

TABLE 6.2
Two-Stage Swamy Estimates for the Regression of Diplomatic
Friendliness on Trade

| | Lagged endogenous included | | Lagged endogenous excluded | |
| | GLS | GLS-ARMA | GLA | GLS-ARMA |
| | | b | | b |
| | (standard error) | | (standard error) | |
|---|---|---|---|---|
| CONSTANT | 1.1157 | .9797 | 1.1322 | .9847 |
| | (.1012) | (.0343) | (.9433) | (.1052) |
| INSTRUMENT FOR TRADE | 1.3631 | 1.3536 | 2.2931 | 2.2994 |
| | (.0085) | (.0061) | (.0088) | (.0033) |
| FRIEND (t-1) | .3840 | .3883 | — | — |
| | (.0035) | (.0025) | | |
| adj. $R^2$ | 1.0 | 1.0 | .998 | .998 |
| $\rho$ | | .002 | | .048 |

other regression coefficients. Since the Swamy estimates are relatively close to the ARMA version of this model, it suggests that autoregression is probably not contaminating this regression model.

## CONCLUSIONS ON TWO-STAGE ESTIMATION[B]

Identification of structural equation models is an important part of building models and estimating parameters. For the under-identified model, identification is frequently accomplished through the addition of instruments, but there are some serious implications from achieving identification in this way. Judge et al. (1985) make the following point in this regard:

The density of the instrumental variable estimator displays more bias as the number of additional instruments used for the $n$ right-hand side endogenous variable increases [p. 613].

In addition to bias, over-identification could also result, and then there is no longer a *unique* solution to the structural equations. In the presence of over-identification, several tests are appropriate.[22]

Often, the instrument is collinear with the included variables, and then the least squares estimator cannot be used. Instead, some other approach to estimation, for example, maximum likelihood techniques, is appropriate. This is still no guarantee that a unique solution to the identification problem can be found. Should multicollinearity plague the regression, even maximum likelihood estimation is not helpful. Two-stage estimation is really not the best solution to endogeneity or nonlinearity in a pool because the underlying error structures are often so complex as to cause intractable problems. On the other hand, there are some relatively simple estimation problems easily managed with maximum likelihood techniques, which are not undermined by a data matrix that combines cross-sections and time series. Among the more widely used models that rely on maximum likelihood estimation are nonlinear models.

## Maximum Likelihood Estimation[B]

The asymptotic properties of least squares estimators in a pooled time series are easily surpassed by maximum likelihood estimators, although the maximum likelihood estimators are not always the estimators of choice. Maximum likelihood estimators are indeed more efficient, but a pool of time series is frequently far too heterogeneous for the question of efficiency to win out over the question of bias. Each pool is unique, but in this section we briefly take up a class of efficient estimators that are particularly valuable when the distributional properties required to use least squares estimators do not apply to the pooled time series. Maximum likelihood is especially advantageous when the distribution of the observed sample is non-normal and the errors are not independent and identically distributed (iid). This arises when there is heteroscedasticity, linear dependence, or autocorrelation.

Maximum likelihood is a method of estimation that produces parameter estimates from an *objective function.* An objective function is a statement of a relationship between a set of independent variables and a dependent variable. Under least squares criteria, an objective function minimizes the sum of squared residual variance from an actual point to a predicted point on a prediction line. The maximum likelihood criterion maximizes the *probability* of generating the sample observed. When the sample contains all of the information necessary to generate the unknown parameters in a regression model, $\beta$ and

$\sigma^2$, we call the method *full information maximum likelihood* (FIML) estimation. The variance-covariance matrix for an FIML estimator is an information matrix whose inverse provides a bound to test significance of the estimates.[23]

The maximum likelihood estimator is derived from an objective function and is determined to be the value where the set of unknown parameters is at a maximum. For example, consider the following objective function:

$$L\,(Y_{nt}\,|\,X_{nt}\,\beta_k) = P\,(Y_{nt}\,|\,X_{nt}). \qquad [6.10]$$

Equation 6.10 states that the likelihood of $Y$ given $X$ is equal to its probability of occurrence in the sample. We now have to make an assumption about the distribution of the sample that is reasonable. This assumption is what makes MAXL and FIML so attractive. If it is known that the sample is not distributed normally, we can set out this assumption beforehand. MAXL is especially attractive when the dependent variable is not continuous, as is often the case when the decision to be analyzed is a choice between discrete categories rather than a value on a continuum.

## LOGIT and PROBIT Specifications[B]

For our example in equation 6.10 above, we are interested in deriving an estimate for two unknown parameters, $\beta$ and $\sigma^2$. Let us subsume these two unknowns into a set of unknowns called $\theta$. The inverse of $\theta$, or $\theta^{-1}$, is an approximation of the variance-covariance matrix for the ML estimator under distributional assumptions. Two of the most common distributional assumptions are that the distribution of $\theta^{-1}$ is normal, which leads to a LOGIT specification, or that $\theta^{-1}$ is distributed as a probability unit (PROBIT).

The choice of LOGIT or PROBIT specifications is a function of the relationship between the normal categories of the dependent variable. In many applied settings, these normal categories reflect choices that are independent of all other choices. This is frequently referred to as the independence or irrelevant alternatives, and it is the assumption of the LOGIT model. The PROBIT model requires no such assumption and for that reason is often the specification of choice. A simple example might suffice to show the difference that the assumption can make. Take, for example, the choice to approve or disapprove of the job that the President is doing at any given point in time.

We could easily assume that these choices are independent of any third alternative in the survey (such as, no opinion), perhaps because there was no third alternative, or, given a third alternative, (independent) individuals would still feel compelled to choose between approval and disapproval. Under this assumption, the LOGIT model would be appropriate. However, if it could be argued that in the presence of a third alternative (no opinion) this new alternative would alter the distribution of the two original choices, then a PROBIT specification would be appropriate. In either case, the models are relatively straightforward.

The LOGIT model characterizes a function of $X'\beta$ such that:

$$F(X_{nt}'\beta_k) = 1/(1 + e^{-x'\beta}). \qquad [6.11]$$

The PROBIT characterizes a function of the following form:

$$F(X_{nt}'\beta_k) = \int_{-\infty}^{X'\beta} (1/\sqrt{2\pi})\varepsilon^{-t^2/2} dt. \qquad [6.12]$$

For the two-choice case, consider the following equation:

$$Y_{nt} = X_{nt}\beta_k + e_{nt}. \qquad [6.13]$$

There are only two possible values for $Y_{nt}$ in this example, but the model can be extended to include more values on the dependent variable.[24] Our goal is to predict to one of these two values from a set of exogenous effects. The qualitative variable model given in equation 6.12 is to be estimated in a pool of time series. We first transform the exogenous variable vector $X'\beta$ into a probability of distribution. We can model the probability of observing one value of $Y_{nt}$ as a function of the exogenous effects and as the probability of observing a set of values for the exogenous effects that index the value on the dependent variable. Consider such a model in the following equation:

$$Pr(Y_{nt} = 1 \mid S_i) = Pr(S^* \le S_i) = F(\chi_{nt}'\beta_k) \qquad [6.14]$$

where $S^*$ is a random variable (or index) that reflects the pool's characteristics. By the central limit theorem, we can assume that $S^*$ is a normally distributed random variable, and so the probability of one value of $Y_{nt}$ occurring is taken as the normal cumulative density function evaluated at its argument. The logistic CDF is often used to approximate the normal CDF because it is numerically simpler.

$$F(X_{nt}'\beta_k) = 1/(1 + \exp(-X_{nt}'\beta_k)) \quad where \ -\infty < X_{nt}'\beta_k < \infty. \qquad [6.15]$$

The alternate choice for the dependent variable is then $1-F(x_{nt}'\beta_k)$, and we can now derive a likelihood function to maximize:

$$L = \Pi \left[ F\left(X_{nt}'\beta_k\right)\right]^Y_{nt} \left[ 1 - F\left(X_{nt}'\beta_k\right)\right]^{1-Y}_{nt}. \qquad [6.16]$$

This function, while apparently simple, is somewhat problematic because we are trying to estimate it in a pool of time series. There are two approaches to estimation under these conditions. First, the nominal categories of the dependent variable (the alternative) might not be allowed to vary from individual cross-section to cross-section and/or time point to time point. In this case, the LOGIT model is an appropriate choice. Yet, it is much more likely that the choices will vary over the cross-sections, but the *choices* may not vary in time. The error in the choices, however, may be correlated in time through an autoregressive process, in which case such a situation could be corrected through standard procedures.

When the $\beta_k$ vary across the time series and/or the cross-sections in a discrete dependent variable model, it is convenient to treat the problem as one that combines continuous and discrete elements. The discrete elements emanate from the dependent variable where the continuous elements emanate from the exogenous effects. A discrete dependent variable model can be estimated with any of the techniques we have examined for continuous dependent variables, except that we no longer have a near continuous function from which to derive estimates of the variance of the estimator. In fact, the distribution is a combination of discrete and continuous functions. In large samples (where $n$ and $t$ are large), this will not pose a problem, but in small samples, maximum likelihood techniques are appropriate. An example of MAXL estimation on diplomatic friendliness is given in Table 6.3. In this table we are estimating the probability that diplomatic friendliness or hostility is significantly different in the presence of trade rather than that probability that would have occurred by chance (in the presence of trade). In the first set of results presented in Table 6.3 below, it is assumed that the choices of individual decision-makers to be friendly or hostile are independent from any third alternative that might reveal itself (e.g., no action), and, moreover, that the choices are basically the same throughout the time series. The choices, however, may vary from cross-section to cross-section (the cross-sections in this data are six nation-states), and the error in time may be correlated. The second set of results does not assume independence of irrelevant alternatives. The PROBIT specification is used in

TABLE 6.3

LOGIT and PROBIT Estimates for the Regression of Presidential
Popularity on Prior Approval

|  | LOGIT<br>b<br>(standard error) | PROBIT<br>b<br>(standard error) |
|---|---|---|
| CONSTANT | 1.9615<br>(.6434) | 1.3670<br>(.7266) |
| FRIEND (t-1) | .3837<br>(.1038) | .4719<br>(.1233) |
| TRADE | 5.1092<br>(1.2303) | 5.8903<br>(1.3712) |
| adj. $R^2$ | .709 | .771 |

column 2 to reflect the presence of a third alternative to influence the probability of the occurrence of the first two alternatives.

For these data, the LOGIT and PROBIT specifications are very close in their estimates of the effect of trade on diplomatic friendliness. The range of the dependent variable was originally 0.0 to 6.11. The arithmetic mean value of 4.2 was used as the threshold value to create the binary variable used in the LOGIT and PROBIT estimations. These data are not contaminated by serial correlation even in the presence of a lag, but it is clear that the nonlinear aspects of the choice for diplomatic friendliness are well served by this nonlinear specification. The $R^2$ cannot be interpreted as a general fit parameter but only as the probability of a particular choice being made. In this example, the dependent variable was divided into two categories of friendliness (high level friendliness represented by values above the mean and low level friendliness represented by values below the mean). The coefficients can be interpreted as the probability of occurrence in one category of friendliness (high or low) given the presence of the variables in the regression equation.

## Conclusions on Maximum Likelihood[B]

In a pool of time series, every complication added to the estimation process is costly in terms of computation time and expense in estimation. Because maximum likelihood is an iterative technique, it can be very costly if the necessity arises for this technique in the course of research. The examples given here are relatively stable in effect across different models because the underlying assumptions are plausible. The empirical estimation only adds to the plausibility of these assumptions. If, in the course of estimation, however, the researcher finds markedly different effects from even slight variations of the same model, she/he would be well advised to reexamine the plausibility of the underlying assumptions. In many instances, a simple correction, such as a nonlinear form, can solve the problem, but in a pool of time series nonlinearity may mask itself in heteroscedasticity and go undiscovered for many rounds of estimation. Perhaps what is most important is the researcher's own confidence in the estimates produced. Thus, the research enterprise is well served by establishing the robustness of the estimates.

## 7. ROBUSTNESS: HOW GOOD ARE THESE ESTIMATES?[A]

Estimating parameters in a pool of time series is one econometric task that cannot be harmed by establishing the robustness of the estimators. Robustness usually refers to the reliability of the derived estimates in the presence of a mistaken assumption, such as the underlying normality of the distribution, dependence of the error on unobserved effects, or misspecifying the structure of the error. We are all familiar with hypothesis testing as a means to establish some support for an underlying theory. Theory could be perfectly valid, and yet, the hypotheses of interest do not support it. Frequently, when this situation arises, some assumption or set of assumptions about the sample is mistaken. We would like then, in the best of all possible worlds, to use statistics and estimators that can be relied on even in the face of mistaken assumptions. These model-fitting statistics, tests of significance, and estimators, because they stand up well against contamination, are called *robust*. In many instances, robustness cannot be assumed but rather should be established in very much the same way that we might establish the power of a test. In the next section, we consider some practical ways to establish the robustness of estimators, tests, and statistics in a pool.

# Robust Estimators[B]

Robustness in a pool is directly related to the residuals. There are several avenues to robustness, but all of them require an examination of the residuals. The central idea is to minimize the contamination from outliers without completely ignoring the influence of these data points. We can trim the residuals by replacing the actual residual value with an estimate. Least squares is not robust against nonnormal disturbances so we are particularly concerned with discounting the residuals in a way that would discount them somewhat more than they are discounted in least squares. Under least squares assumptions, simply standardizing the estimates by normalizing the residuals treats all estimates equally and results in discounting the residuals in constant proportions. I hope that by this point in the discussion it has become perhaps painfully obvious that such an assumption is not particularly useful in pooled time series. Each cross-section deserves to contribute to total contamination in a unique way. Trimming residuals to establish more robust estimates attempts to uncover these unique contributions by sorting out which residuals should be discounted more than others. For example, Huber's (1981) approach assigns an arbitrary value to residuals that fall outside of the bounds of the specified distribution. This approach to trimming has been called *winsorizing* the residuals.

## WINSORIZING RESIDUALS

Winsorizing residuals is a trimming technique that redistributes the contaminating effects closer to a hypothesized distribution. In application, Huber (1981) suggests a pseudo maximum likelihood technique to generate the winsorized residuals, but luckily a computationally simpler technique will also work. Judge et al. (1985:831) recommend using a standard measure of dispersion for the residuals to set the threshold or cutoff value for winsorizing, such as the absolute value of the median of the residuals. Consider the following equation to winsorize residuals:

$$U^* = -c\sigma \text{ if } Y - X'\beta < -c\sigma \qquad [7.1]$$

$$= u \text{ if } Y - X'\beta \le -c\sigma$$

$$= c\,\sigma \text{ if } Y - X'\beta > c\sigma$$

TABLE 7.1

Winsorized Residuals for OLS and Two-Stage Residuals from the
Regression of Diplomatic Friendliess on Trade

| | OLS Residuals | | | Two-Stage Residuals | |
| --- | --- | --- | --- | --- | --- |
| | Original | Winsorized | | Original | Winsorized |
| | .826 | .8034 | | 2.723 | .7732 |
| | −.532 | −.5317 | | −0.547 | −,5471 |
| | −.078 | −.0785 | | .417 | .4167 |
| | −.078 | −.0785 | | .060 | .0599 |
| | .748 | .7484 | | −1.014 | .7732 |
| | −.583 | −.5834 | | −0.560 | −.5600 |
| | .984 | .8034 | | 1.396 | .7732 |
| | .316 | .3163 | | .235 | .2353 |
| | −.330 | −.3305 | | −0.193 | −.1929 |
| | −.532 | −.5315 | | −0.224 | −.2241 |
| σ | .5356 | | | .5155 | |
| c | 1.5 | | | 1.5 | |

Judge et al. (1985:831) suggest that the constant $c$ is usually taken to be about 1.5 reflecting normal distributional assumptions. In this capacity, $\sigma$ has no substantive interpretation but works in a statistical sense to trim the residuals. The value of $\sigma$ is chosen arbitrarily, for example, as the median value of the residuals, and can be used to start the iterative process that solves the maximum likelihood equation. This value could easily be generated from a least squares or ARMA estimate. When the estimates of $\sigma$ converge asymptotically, we have arrived at a maximum likelihood solution for the value at which to trim the residuals. Table 7.1 shows values for winsorized residuals as compared with OLS residuals for the diplomatic friendliness data.

The residuals in this table are trimmed, and the impact of trimming is given in Table 7.2 where OLS and winsorized OLS estimates on diplomatic friendliness are compared. The results show an increase in the strength of the effects and the general fit. Another example of the impact of winsorizing is given in Table 7.3 for the same data, but under a two-stage structural model. The original two-stage estimates are compared with the winsorized estimates. Perhaps most impressive from these comparisons is the robustness or stability of these coefficients. Winsorizing can be a valuable check on heteroscedasticity and contamination from outliers.

TABLE 7.2

OLS and Winsorized OLS Estimates for the Regression of
Diplomatic Friendliness on Trade

|  | OLS<br>b<br>(standard error) | Winsorized OLS<br>b<br>(standard error) |
|---|---|---|
| CONSTANT | 2.4764<br>(.2067) | 1.5015<br>(.6006) |
| TRADE | 4.0546<br>(.4137) | 8.9898<br>(.0470) |
| adj. $R^2$<br>pooled | .399 | .996 |
| Durbin-Watson<br>d | 1.23 | 1.63 |

TABLE 7.3

Two-Stage GLS and Winsorized Two-Stage GLS Estimates for the
Regression of Diplomatic Friendliness on Trade

|  | GLS | | | |
|---|---|---|---|---|
|  | ORIGINAL | | WINSORIZED | |
|  | Lagged endogenous | | | |
|  | included | excluded | included | excluded |
|  | b | | b | |
|  | (standard error) | | (standard error) | |
| CONSTANT | 1.1157<br>(.1012) | 1.1322<br>(.9433) | 1.4684<br>(.1199) | 1.4892<br>(.9461) |
| INSTRUMENT<br>FOR TRADE | 1.3631<br>(.0085) | 2.2931<br>(.0088) | 1.3633<br>(.0100) | 2.2933<br>(.0088) |
| FRIEND (t-1) | .3840<br>(.0035) |  | .3840<br>(.0041) |  |
| adj. $R^2$ | 1.0 | .998 | 1.0 | .998 |

## Heteroscedasticity and Robustness[A]

Robustness of an estimator is undermined by outliers in the residuals, but contamination also arises from systematic sources of non-constant variance, i.e., heteroscedasticity. In a pool of time series, certain series and, often, groups of series may nullify the assumption of homoscedastic errors. Tests for heteroscedasticity are very useful because they can aid in identifying the source of contamination. One approach to identifying sources of contamination is to select at random time series and compare the variance of one series to other series in the pool. It is often now a common feature of statistical software to have a random number function that can be easily utilized to generate time series at random (especially when the number of time series is large). We can remove one series at a time from the pool and re-estimate the regression model each time a series is removed. When we compare the estimates derived by this technique, which is termed *jackknifing*, we can establish the robustness of the derived estimates.

### JACKKNIFING[B]

Jackknifing, however, is an approach that does not yield a statistically conclusive result concerning the source or effect of the contaminating series, despite the time it takes to jackknife. In a pool of time series, it is frequently the case that contamination results not from a single series but from an entire cross-section of series. In this case, modified jackknifing can be used, which pulls entire series at a time to consider the sensitivity of the estimates under the assumptions of different regression models. In Table 7.4, jackknifed estimates for the OLS, LSDV, and Swamy models are compared. No unit effects are reported for the LSDV because of space considerations.

The comparison in Table 7.4 reveals the lack of robustness in the effects for the LSDV model, but the OLS and Swamy models perform very well across the different cross-sections. One exception emerges for case number 740, which is Japan. This effect is likely to have been produced from Japan's relatively new status as a major trade partner (recall that this time series dates back to 1950). Still jackknifing is only a guide to contamination and robustness and should be considered in conjunction with more statistically derived tests, such as the Goldfeld-Quandt test used earlier on in this monograph (see Chapter 3). Let us take up this topic once again to illustrate the im-

TABLE 7.4
Jackknifed Estimates for the Regression of
Diplomatic Friendliness on Trade

| | OLS b (standard error) | LSDV b (standard error) | Swamy-GLS b (standard error) |
|---|---|---|---|
| CONSTANT (without) | | | |
| US | 1.4505(.0539) | — | 2.9065(.6480) |
| CAN | 1.7287(.2958) | — | 3.0612(.5787) |
| UK | 1.6402(.2823) | — | 2.8358(.6639) |
| FRN | 1.6827(.2932) | — | 2.9048(.6464) |
| ITA | 1.6512(.2902) | — | 3.0328(.6538) |
| JAP | 2.0851(.3459) | — | 3.9234(.6576) |
| | | | |
| TRADE (without) | | | |
| US | 2.8463(.1029) | .9899(.6892)* | 3.4889(2.0688) |
| CAN | 1.7287(.2950) | 1.1686(.5535) | 3.2053(1.2014) |
| UK | 3.1530(.5072) | 1.1301(.6898) | 3.0882(1.5496) |
| FRN | 2.9197(.5283) | 1.0166(.7255)* | 2.8116(1.5532) |
| ITA | 3.0757(.5360) | .8575(.7679)* | 2.7592(1.4701) |
| JAP | 2.5797(.5522) | .0941(.7718)* | 1.1957(1.4551)* |
| | | | |
| FRIEND (t-1) (without) | | | |
| US | .3730(.0148) | .1445(.0893) | .2613(.1137) |
| CAN | .3482(.0741) | .1115(.0795) | .2760(.1037) |
| UK | .2692(.0789) | .0984(.0829)* | .2610(.1243) |
| FRN | .2942(.0791) | .0960(.0831)* | .2439(.1129) |
| ITA | .2903(.0799) | .0807(.0835)* | .2162(.1180) |
| JAP | .2723(.0810) | .0348(.0827)* | .1434(.1163)* |

*These estimates are not robust because they are not statistically significant.

Unit effects for LSDV model not included because of space considerations.

portance of heteroscedasticity tests for establishing the robustness of the estimates.

## HETEROSCEDASTICITY TESTS[A]

Goldfeld and Quandt (1972) recommend a simple but statistically useful test to uncover heteroscedasticity. First, order the observations (in this case the series) with respect to their variance. Each cross-section will contain a time series, and cross-sections with small variance over time will be sorted out from cross-sections with large variance over time. We can also sort variance by year then order by all cross-sections (within a particular year) with the smallest variance to cross-sections with the largest variance. The Goldfeld and Quandt test excludes some observations in the middle in order to assume independence between the residuals in the ratio of the two sets of observations.[25] We can then use a restricted F test from the two separate regressions to establish the heteroscedasticity. For an $n$ of cases $= 30$, Goldfeld and Quandt omit four observations.

In a pool, the number of omitted observations is not intuitively obvious to derive. Because a pool is actually *stacks of heteroscedasticity*, both individual time series and groups of series should be tested as sources of contamination. The pool should first be sorted by nondecreasing variance and if the theoretical justification exists to exclude groups of series, then groups should be excluded. For example, when we considered the LSDV model, we suggested that a dummy variable might capture some of the variance left unexplained by the exogenous effects. As a source of contamination, the same effects that could be captured by dummy variables can and should be tested against the null hypothesis of homoscedasticity. This is a very simple but very attractive way to test the robustness of the coefficients derived under the LSDV model. In our example, we might consider excluding the 1950s from the presidential popularity data because of anti-Communist sentiment and the "rally 'round the flag" effects of that particular time period.

Suppose that no theoretical reason is immediately apparent? Then it is still appropriate to exclude a small number of observations (groups of series) from the center of the variance order. This kind of test, like other ratio tests for heteroscedasticity, falls into a class of tests characterized by Szroeter (1978), where the test statistic can be used in a manner similar to the Durbin-Watson statistic in uncovering autocorrelation. Like the Durbin-Watson test statistic, however, the inconclusive region for the Szroeter test statistic makes it difficult to reject the null hypothesis. The ratio tests like that of Goldfeld and Quandt (1972) or Thiel (1971) do not guarantee conclusive evidence of the detection of heteroscedasticity, but they are an important part of the detection process. Examine the test results reported for the presidential popularity data in Table 7.5.

Both the more computationally complex Bartlett test and the Goldfeld-Quandt test reveal heteroscedasticity for these data. The ratio in

TABLE 7.5

Heteroscedasticity Test Results for Regression of Presidential
Popularity on Prior Approval

| YEAR | $\sigma^2$ | $ln(\sigma^2)$ | $ln(\sigma^2)*(Ti-1)$ |
|------|------|------|------|
| 1984 | .0001 | −9.91 | −101.30 |
| 1960 | .0002 | −8.52 | − 93.69 |
| 1965 | .0002 | −8.52 | − 93.69 |
| 1954 | .0003 | −8.11 | − 89.23 |
| 1958 | .0003 | −8.11 | − 89.23 |
| 1970 | .0003 | −8.11 | − 89.23 |
| 1959 | .0004 | −7.82 | − 86.07 |
| 1962 | .0004 | −7.82 | − 86.07 |
| 1982* | .0004 | −7.82 | − 86.07 |
| 1978* | .0009 | −7.01 | − 77.14 |
| 1983 | .0010 | −6.91 | − 75.99 |
| 1966 | .0014 | −6.57 | − 72.28 |
| 1967 | .0015 | −6.50 | − 71.53 |
| 1969 | .0022 | −6.12 | − 67.31 |
| 1973 | .0031 | −5.78 | − 63.54 |
| 1979 | .0067 | −5.01 | − 55.06 |
| 1981 | .0080 | −4.83 | − 53.11 |
| 1974 | .0177 | −4.03 | − 44.38 |

$\Sigma 1 = .0451$ $\Sigma 2 = -1394.92$

Goldfeld-Quandt R = (residual sum of squares (second half))/(residual sum of squares (first half)).

Bartlett's M = $((T - m)R1 - (T_i - 1)R2)/1 + (.33(m - 1)) * (m(1/T_i - 1) - 1/(T - m)$
where: T = 216; Ti = 12; m = 18).

Goldfeld-Quandt R = 8.9101/.4126 = 21.595 (reject $H_0$ = homoscedasticity)
Bartlett's M = 148.73 · (reject $H_0$ = homoscedasticity)

*Omitted for Goldfeld-Quandt test.

the Goldfeld-Quandt test is one where the numerator contains the larger variance in the pool. In this example, the tests clearly indicate rejection of the null hypothesis of homoscedasticity.

It is easy to see that robustness is not easily established, even with statistical tests against heteroscedasticity available. Unless the test is very precise in specifying the exact form of the heteroscedasticity, these tests can usually only confirm suspicions the researcher already has about the heteroscedasticity in the pool. Yet, they are important because we too often worry over autoregression when the contaminant effects from the cross-sections are many times more devastating to estimation. Because of the presence of information over time and across space, some stochastic process is likely to be present, but the stochastic process is usually heteroscedastic rather than homoscedastic. These tests are useful in OLS models, but their utility diminishes as the models take on more complex, in particular, stochastic characters. Engle (1982) has proposed a modified Lagrange multiplier test, which is widely used for random coefficient models to establish the robustness of stochastic parameters (Newbold and Bos, 1985). The test statistic is $TR_2$ where $T$ is the number of cases and $R^2$ is the regression fit statistic (multiple correlation coefficient squared) from a two-stage regression.[26]

It is also worthwhile to consider that the structure of the covariance matrix may be amenable to transformation by a relatively simple technique (such as a log transformation) as long as the disturbances can be characterized as additive or multiplicative. For example, the Box-Cox transformation is widely used to transform nonlinear residuals. It corrects for multiplicative disturbances and is applied with relative ease.[27]

# 8. CONCLUSIONS ON POOLED TIME SERIES[A]

It was Seneca who said, "When a man does not know for which harbor he is heading, no wind is the right wind." I find this advice most appropriate to using pooled time series designs. There are so many potential problems to contend with in a pool that it is not surprising much of this monograph has been spent on the theoretical aspects of the pooled estimators and tests to uncover contamination. A pool is a combination of the problems of time series and the problems of cross-sectional analysis. Needless to say, our models and theories should be as well specified as possible, and, after that, the residuals will yield most of the information necessary to detect and correct problems in the pool.

The pooled time series design has gained a great deal of popularity because so many of the questions social and behavioral scientists are interested in are questions about variation in time as well as in space. Yet, the pooled design can quickly become a barrier to answering those questions if thoughtful consideration is not given beforehand to the *meaning* of the aggregations in the pool. Some pooled researchers will have a great deal of experience in estimating time series and be less sensitive to cross-sectional variation and the problems it can cause. Others will be more used to estimation in cross-sections and have little feel for how autoregressive or moving average processes work.

This monograph was an effort to explicate some techniques currently available to estimate regression models in a pool of cross-sections and time series. There are many topics not included in this monograph that could be very valuable to the modeler, but they are somewhat beyond the scope of this monograph. For most problems that the applied researcher in social and behavioral science would confront, the regression models described herein are sufficient. For some problems, however, conditional heteroscedasticity models and more complex versions of random coefficient or stochastic parameter models should be utilized. Indeed, finding the *best* model is the most difficult problem of all, but it is also the simplest because it turns out that for most applications the heterogeneity of the pool makes least squares estimators the most tractable way to derive believable parameters that make sense and can be substantively interpreted.

# NOTES

1. As Stimson (1985) accurately points out, pooled designs are frequently referred to as panel designs. I would like to distinguish pooled designs from panel designs. I treat panel designs as a set of cross-sectional observations at various points in time that are not necessarily contiguous in time. A panel might thus consist of observations from 1960, 1965, 1970, 1975. I do not refer to these panels as series because, in the standard usage of the term "series," a series is thought to be contiguous in the fixed interval of the time sequence.

2. Analysis of interrupted time series and forecasting models such as Box-Jenkins, for example, may require at least fifty time points depending on how the lag structure is specified.

3. For good reviews on these topics the interested reader is directed to Ostrom's (1978) Sage monograph on time series techniques, Lewis-Beck's (1980) monograph on regression, and Achen's (1982) monograph on interpreting and using regression.

4. The first paper on this topic appears to be Howles (1950) discussion paper.

5. A covariance technique is defined as any method that minimizes the covariance (unexplained variation associated with explained variation between one cross-section and another) in the data rather than the unexplained variation within the cross-section associated with explained variation. The $X_i$ has the same relationship to $Y_i$ between the cross-sections, just one of a different magnitude or direction.

6. When the number of cases is modest in size, the estimated variance in the sample is not reliable.

7. Tests for first order or higher order autoregression can be made cross-section by cross-section. The pooled statistic Stimson (1985) recommends is simply an average of individual series statistics. Tests for heteroscedastic errors must be made on the full pool. See Judge et al. (1985) and especially Chapter 11 of that text for a full discussion of alternative tests for heteroscedasticity. When we consider the random coefficient model in Chapter 5, more detailed examples of these test procedures are given.

8. The researcher may test for a first-order process on a cross-section by cross-section basis. Define the Durbin d as the appropriate test statistic for individual time series within the cross-section. This statistic can then be used to correct for the autoregression cross-section by cross-section.

9. The Theil (1971) test uses a ratio of the first half of the series residuals to the second half, which has an $F$ distribution under the null hypothesis that the $U_{it}$ are independent and identically distributed (iid) with a mean of zero and constant variance labeled $\sigma^2$. If OLS residuals are used as estimates of the true disturbances, the numerator and denominator are not iid. In this case, the Goldfeld and Quandt (1965) test statistic is appropriate.

10. I would like to thank James Stimson who has kindly allowed me to use these data here as reproduced from the American National Election Survey.

11. If the $X$ vector contains variables that are time invariant, they are not separable from the effects of the dummies and are eliminated by the dummy variable estimator (Chamberlain, 1978; Hausman and Taylor, 1981; Judge et al., 1985).

12. The interested reader is directed to Chamberlain (1978; 1983), Chamberlain and Griliches (1975), and Hausman and Taylor (1981) for efficient estimation under these conditions.

13. These data are generated from Azar's (1980) Conflict and Peace Data Bank by Brian Pollins, to whom I am indebted for allowing me to use them here. The diplomatic friendliness score is derived as the proportion of friendly activity over total activity (conflict plus cooperation).

14. Robustness is defined as a characteristic of an estimator that is efficient in minimizing the sum of squared errors without an underlying distribution that is assumed to be standard normal. Robustness is endangered by heterogeneity, autoregression, and/or nonlinearity.

15.
$$\rho^2 g (1 - \rho)^2 = \sigma_v^2$$
$$(1 - \rho)^2 = \sigma_v^2 / s_g^2$$
$$1 - \rho = \sigma_v / \sigma_g$$
$$\rho = 1 - (\sigma_v / \sigma_g)$$

16. $\rho = 1 - (\sigma_v / \sigma_g)$.

17. Exogenous refers to effects that are stochastically independent of the disturbances from the regression equation(s). Endogenous variables are determined by both the exogenous variables and the disturbances in the regression equation(s). These terms are introduced here because they are appropriate to dynamic specifications and systems-of-equations like the Zellner SUR model. Even though we are not utilizing the SUR model as a system-of-equations model in the strict sense, we are utilizing it in such a way as to make the identification of the pooled regression in terms of the exogenous and endogenous variables a necessary condition to the application of this model.

18. A stationary process is a stochastic process where the mean, variance, and covariances are finite and the covariance between $Y_t$ and $Y_{t+1}$ does not depend on any single time point $t$.

19. One approximating function that is increasingly gaining attention is the cubic spline. In the cubic spline, the "knots" (joining points) are known and the transition between regimes is smooth.

20. Orthogonality and singularity are terms of matrix mathematics. Orthogonality refers to the vector elements of a matrix whereby for two vectors, $X$ and $Y$, if $X'Y = Y'X = 0$ and $X'X \neq Y'Y \neq 0$, $X$ and $Y$ are said to be orthogonal. A nonsingular matrix is one where the determinant exists and is not equal to zero, thus making the matrix invertible (Johnston, 1972:104).

21. There are several excellent treatments of the identification problem currently available in Econometric texts, including Wonnacott and Wonnacott (1970) and Judge et al. (1985: Chapter 14).

22. Judge et al. (1985:614-616) discuss several tests for over-identification, including likelihood ratio tests.

23. The bound is actually the Cramer-Rao lower bound, and it is equal to the variance of an unbiased estimator such as MAXL or FIML. The FIML and MAXL estimators are most efficient in a class of estimators called MVUE, a minimum variance unbiased estimator. See White (1984) for the full proof.

24. Extensions of this model include the multinominal LOGIT and PROBIT, but they also include more complex discrete choice, e.g., as a function of an underlying principle of choice like utility maximization or as the prediction of anticipated values (thresholds).

25. If the middle observations are not excluded, the ratio would not have an F distribution under the null hypothesis of homoscedasticity (Theil, 1971).

26. Again, this is taken from Engle's (1982) discussion of the ARCH model, and the interested reader is directed to that paper for a further development of this statistic.

27. The Box-Cox transformation is as follows:

$Y_{nt} = X_{nt} b_k + e_{nt}$

where $Y_{nt} = (Y_{nt})^{\varphi - 1} / \theta$.

Thus, $\ln(Y_{nt})^{\varphi - 1} = \ln Y_{nt}$.

# REFERENCES

ACHEN, C. H. (1982) Interpreting and Using Regression. Sage University Series Paper on Quantitative Applications in the Social Sciences, 07-029. Beverly Hills, CA: Sage.

ACHEN, C. H. (1986) "Necessary and sufficient conditions for unbiased aggregation of cross-sectional regressions." Paper presented at the Third Annual Methodology Conference, Harvard University, Cambridge, MA, August 7-10, 1986.

AMEMIYA, T. (1985) Advanced Econometrics. Cambridge, MA: Harvard University Press.

AZAR, E. E. (1980) The Codebook of the Conflict and Peace Data Bank. Chapel Hill: University of North Carolina at Chapel Hill.

BALESTRA, P. and M. NERLOVE (1966) "Pooling cross section and time series data in the estimation of a dynamic model: The demand for natural gas." Econometrica 34(3):585-612.

BARTLETT, M. S. (1937) "Properties of sufficiency and statistical tests." Proceedings of the Royal Society (Series A) 160: 268-282.

CHAMBERLAIN, G. (1978) "Omitted variable bias in panel data: Estimating the returns to schooling." Annales de L'Insee 30/31:49-82.

CHAMBERLAIN, G. (1983) "Multivariate regression models for panel data." Journal of Econometrics 18(1982):5-46.

CHAMBERLAIN, G. and Z. GRILICHES (1975) "Unobservables with a variance-components structure: Ability, schooling and the economic success of brothers." International Economic Review 16(2):422-450.

ENGLE, R. (1982) "Autoregressive conditional heteroscedasticity with estimates of UK inflations." Econometrica 50(4): 987-1008.

GOLDFELD, S. M. and R. E. QUANDT (1965) "Some tests for homoscedasticity." Journal of the American Statistical Association 60(2):539-547.

GOLDFELD, S. M. and R. E. QUANDT (1972) Nonlinear Methods in Econometrics. Amsterdam: North-Holland.

HAUSMAN, J. A. and W. E. TAYLOR (1981) "Panel data and unobservable individual effects." Econometrica 43(4):1377-1398.

HIBBS, D. A., Jr. (1976) "Industrial conflict in advanced industrial societies." American Political Science Review 70(4):1033-1058.

HOCH, I. (1962) "Estimation of production function parameters combining time-series and cross-section data." Econometrica 30(1):34-53.

HOWLES, C. (1950) "Combining cross-section data and time series." Cowles Commission Discussion Paper, Statistics No 347.

HSAIO, C. (1975) "Some estimation methods for a random coefficient model." Econometrica 43(2):305-325.

HUBER, P. J. (1981) Robust Statistics. New York: John Wiley.

JOHNSTON, J. (1972) Econometric Methods. New York: McGraw-Hill.

JUDGE. G. G., W. E. GRIFFITHS, R. C. HILL, H. LUTKEPOHL, and T. C. LEE (1985) The Theory and Practice of Econometrics (2nd ed.). New York: John Wiley.

78

KMENTA, J. (1971) Elements of Econometrics. New York: Macmillan.

LEWIS-BECK, M. (1980) Applied Regression: An Introduction. Sage University Series Paper on Quantitative Applications in the Social Sciences, 07-022. Beverly Hills, CA: Sage.

MADDALA, G. S. (1971) "The use of variance components in pooling cross section and time series data." Econometrica 39(2):341-358.

MADDALA, G. S. (1977) Econometrics. New York: McGraw Hill.

MALVINAUD, E. (1970) Statistical Methods of Econometrics. Amsterdam: North-Holland.

MARKUS, G. B. (1986) "The impact of personal and national economic conditions on the presidential vota: A pooled cross-sectional analysis." Paper presented at the Third Annual Methodology Conference, Harvard University, Cambridge, MA, August 7-10, 1986.

MUNDLAK, Y. (1978) "On the pooling of time series and cross-section data." Econometrica 46(1):69-85.

NERLOVE, M. (1971) "Further evidence on the estimation of dynamic economic relations from a time series of cross sections." Econometrica 39(2):359-382.

NEWBOLD, P. and T. BOS (1985) Stochastic Parameter Regression Models. Sage University Series Paper on Quantitative Applications in the Social Sciences, 07-051. Beverly Hills, CA: Sage.

OSTROM, C. W., Jr. (1978) Time Series Analysis: Regression Techniques. Sage University Series Paper on Quantitative Applications in the Social Sciences, 07-009. Beverly Hills, CA: Sage.

STIMSON, J. A. (1985) "Regression in space and time: A statistical essay." American Journal of Political Science 29(4):914-947.

SWAMY, P. A. V. B. (1970). "Efficient inference in a random coefficient regression model." Econometrica 38(2):311-323.

SZROETER, J. (1978) "A class of parametric tests for heteroscedasticity in linear econometric models." Econometrica 46(4):1311-1328.

THEIL, H. (1971) Principles of Econometrics. New York: John Wiley.

WALLACE, T. D. and A. HUSSEIN (1969) "The use of error components models in combining cross section with time series data." Econometrica 37(1):55-72.

WARD, M. D. (1987) "Cargo cult science and eight fallacies of comparative political research." International Studies Notes 13(3):75-77.

WHITE, H. (1984) Asymptotic Theory for Econometricians. New York: Academic.

WONNACOTT, R. J. and T. H. WONNACOTT (1970) Econometrics. New York: John Wiley.

ZELLNER, A. (1962) "An efficient method of estimating seemingly unrelated regressions and tests of aggregation bias." Journal of the American Statistical Association 57(2):348-368.

ZUK, G. and W. R. THOMPSON (1982) "The post-coup military spending question: A pooled cross-sectional time series analysis." American Political Science Review 76(1):60-74.

*LOIS W. SAYRS is Assistant Professor of Political Science at the University of Iowa. Her Ph.D. is in Political Science from Northwestern University. Her current research interests include discrete choice models of international conflict processes and international political economy.*